RiPPLE 2024

A KINGSTON UNIVERSITY STUDENT ANTHOLOGY

20TH EDITION

RiPPLE 2024

A KINGSTON UNIVERSITY STUDENT ANTHOLOGY

THE 2024 RiPPLE TEAM

KINGSTON UNIVERSITY PRESS

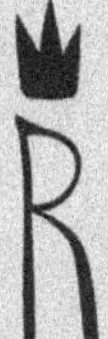

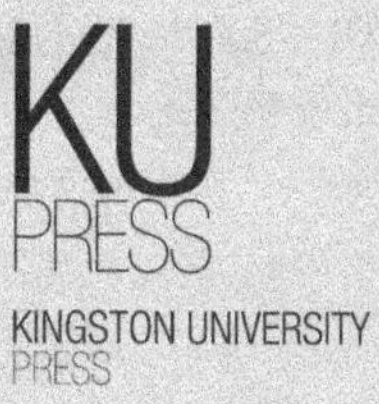

First published in 2024 by Kingston University Press

A catalogue of this book is available from the British Library

ISBN 978-1-909362-76-5
Typeset in Georgia

Cover illustration by Eylul Oguz.
Editorial and Design by Kingston School of Art MA Students

KINGSTON UNIVERSITY PRESS
Kingston University
Penrhyn Road
Kingston-upon-Thames
KT1 2EE

www.kingstonripple.wordpress.com
Instagram account: @ripple_kingston

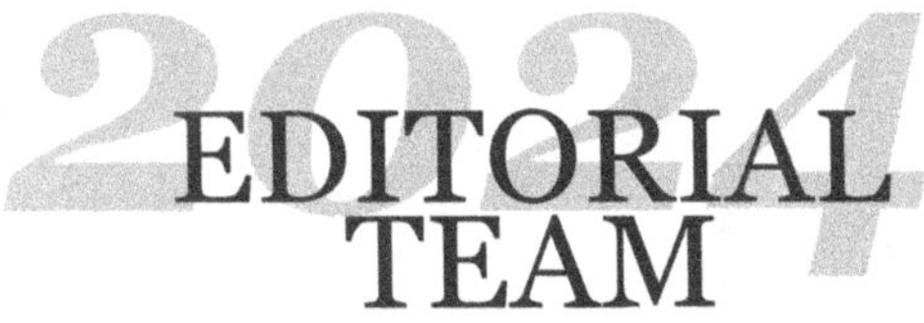

MANAGING EDITOR
Julieta Pereyra

SENIOR COPY EDITOR
Reyna Cox

JUDGES
Alana Applewhaite
Kosha Champaneri
Chaya Chudasama
Reyna Cox
Imogen Crockford
Kassandra Darnell
Rose Edwards
Baz Gibbons
Annie Harris
Han Ilett
Saumya Malik
Ally McAlpine
Karina Miriklis
Annie Monge
Snehakshi Nandy
Verónica S Rodríguez García

COPY EDITORS
Chaya Chudasama
Reyna Cox
Kassandra Darnell
Baz Gibbons
Annie Harris
Han Ilett
Saumya Malik
Annie Monge
Snehakshi Nandy

PROOFREADERS
Chaya Chudasama
Reyna Cox
Imogen Crockford

KU PRESS PUBLISHING ASSISTANT
Yasmien Ibrahim

DESIGN TEAM

ART DIRECTOR
Karina Miriklis

COVER DESIGN
Imogen Crockford

PAGE DESIGN
Chaya Chudasama
Rose Edwards

TYPESETTING TEAM
Chaya Chudasama
Reyna Cox
Kara Daniel
Rose Edwards
Ally McAlpine

POSTER DESIGN
Qingyun Wang

CREATIVE PANEL
Chaya Chudasama
Reyna Cox
Imogen Crockford
Kara Daniel
Ally McAlpine
Qingyun Wang

EBOOK DESIGN
Chaya Chudasama

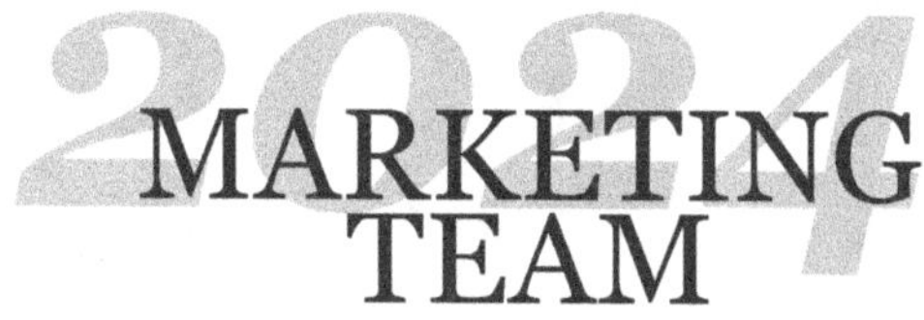

2024 MARKETING TEAM

MARKETING MANAGER
Leah Armstrong

PUBLICITY TEAM
Kara Daniel
Karla Jaime
Ally McAlpine
Kirsten Oshodi-Glover

CANVASSING
Reyna Cox
Kara Daniel
Karla Jaime
Ally McAlpine
Snehakshi Nandy
Verónica S Rodríguez García

PODCAST TEAM
Kara Daniel
Karla Jaime
Ally McAlpine

AUDIOBOOK TEAM
Ally McAlpine
Julieta Pereyra
Verónica S Rodríguez García

2024

CONTENTS

2024 FOREWORD

Dear writer,

Over a decade ago, I flipped through the pages of RiPPLE, in a hurry to see my story in print. It was a particularly touching moment for me, because I had almost lost my chance. Due to challenges I was facing, I was late to reply to the email asking for permission to publish my accepted works. But in the end, they found room for my flash fiction piece and I felt seen, I felt honoured and I felt proud. I still have a copy of that issue of RiPPLE. It was one of those moments that assured me that maybe, just maybe, I could pull this writing thing off.

I am so pleased the publication is alive, kicking and continuing to give writers a platform. Congratulations to those of you included in this edition – may this be the first of many accomplishments. And as for those of you who submitted and were not published, do not despair. Remember, art is subjective and rejection is common. Continue to hone your craft, continue to submit your work and continue to allow yourself to be vulnerable.

I wish you all the best,

Oyinkan Braithwaite
Author of international bestseller, *My Sister, the Serial Killer*
Crime and Thriller Book of the Year, British Book Awards 2020

EPHEMERAL REVERIE

JAD AL SHARAA

In a café in London.

The autumn breeze whispered its chill against my skin, leaving me feeling exposed and vulnerable to its erraticism. In this unfamiliar territory I have little experience with–especially not with You–I took my place early, settling into a seat no different from the others. My gaze aimlessly drifted, awkwardly observing the bustling waitstaff. I hoped to remain indefinitely unnoticed in my solitude. The tapestry of affectionate couples and pensive intellectuals painted the surrounding crowd, their lives wreathed in convoluted patterns, painting a beautiful portrait which I awkwardly centred.

Amidst everyone else, there you stood–a picture of confusion and unease. A mix of conflicting emotions washed over me as I waved in your direction–happiness and sadness entwined at the sight of your short-awaited arrival. However, lost among the shifting sea of faces, you failed to notice me. To you, I was just another anonymous figure, my eyes and features devoid of significance in your eyes, ordinarily common and lost among many. Summoning my resolve, I rose from my seat and approached you, lightly tapping your shoulder. As you turned around, a forced smile curved your lips–a hollow pretence of happiness despite our mutual lack of familiarity. In that moment, I, too, wore a smile–not for you, but because you had shown up. It was reassuring to see you there, yet deep down, a part of me wished you had remained oblivious to my wave, maintaining the comforting distance that surrounded me. I took you to my table, but I couldn't help but feel a slight pang of resentment, as if you were claiming ownership of the table that had kept me company during my period of short but anticipative wait. A small part of me entertained the notion of spending the rest of the evening alone, finding solace in the inanimate object before me–a table that would never disappoint.

Taking my place, my gaze fixated upon you, searching for familiarity, for traits I had longed for. It wasn't that you lacked uniqueness; it was that I didn't want to find anything unique about you. In my heart, I longed for you to resemble traits alien to you, to say phrases you'd probably never heard of, to make hand movements not many even would recognise. You spoke, and I listened. Words flowed effortlessly from your lips while I remained silent, content with my own natural assumption of a quiet audience. I appreciated that you needed no assistance in averting the impending awkward silence that could have made this encounter even more unbearable.

Interrupting, I asked, 'So, how do you like your coffee?' My breath held as I awaited your response. It was only then, to my surprise, that I discovered your disdain for coffee–a revelation that caught me off guard, unveiling yet another layer of unfamiliarity between us, one I could hardly overlook, if I can.

Few minutes pass.

Two cups of latte arrived; my senses swirled in an overwhelming whirlwind, the waiter's words becoming a blur. 'Excuse me,' I interjected, trying to regain composure, 'I ordered an herbal tea for my fr—' My sentence trailed off as I realised you were no longer there.

'I... I am sorry I do not know where he has gone,' I said nervously. Then, just as I had always remembered you, there you were. Your smile, your flowing blonde hair, and that favourite floral shirt of yours. You took your seat at the table, effortlessly plucking the cup of latte from the tray and bringing it to your lips. In that moment, you looked radiant, and I was left utterly speechless. I longed to express my longing, but the words eluded me.

It was clear to me then, as you settled into that chair, that it was meant for you and you alone. 'I missed you,' I found myself repeating. Your reaction was not one of amusement, but your voice held a comforting undertone as you echoed, 'I know.'

You continued to sip your latte, and I wished that the cup would never empty. I yearned for time to stand still, to live out the rest of my days in that eternal moment on that cherished table with you. You placed the latte back on the table, its contents dwindling after a few inconsistent sips. 'I must go,' you remarked, breaking the spell that had enveloped us. 'Your friend might return soon.' Friend? In that moment, everything before you faded into obscurity, and I made a solemn promise to myself to forget anything that would follow. All I desired was for you to stay, to remain in that very place, for as long as it existed, and for long as we existed.

You rose from your seat, and as I looked at you, it felt as though we had returned to that restaurant on the night we first met. You were as captivatingly beautiful as I remembered. Our eyes met, and I saw within yours a flicker of ambition and hope, as if you gazed at me with an abounding love, eagerly anticipating our return home after savouring our desserts.

In that poignant gaze, I found my voice, whispering, 'We never made it, did we?' The fork you held clinked against the table as you replied, 'No. Hey now, please forget about me. Move on.'

I rise slowly from my seat, my steps heavy, and make my way to the restroom to wash my face. When I return to our table and see it empty like I had left it. With a deep breath, I settle the bill and step outside into the relentless downpour, the raindrops mingling with my tears and soaking my coat, mirroring the desolation within, and the distance in between, for one more night.

UNWELCOME PALIMPSEST

BETTY WATERS

I woke to find the snow of love
had fallen silently and densely overnight,
rendering the familiar unrecognisable.
A welcome palimpsest,

perhaps, on clean-slate ground
but here? The enigmatic white,
tantalising as diamonds,
shadows brought cavities to light.

Taking a shovel to it, I found,
to my surprise and delight,
underwritten, in hexagonal crystals,
the permafrost of an older love;

Deeply bonded, anchoring
soul to soul and to this soil,
resolute as concrete.
Stubbornly refusing to thaw.

WINTER NIGHT

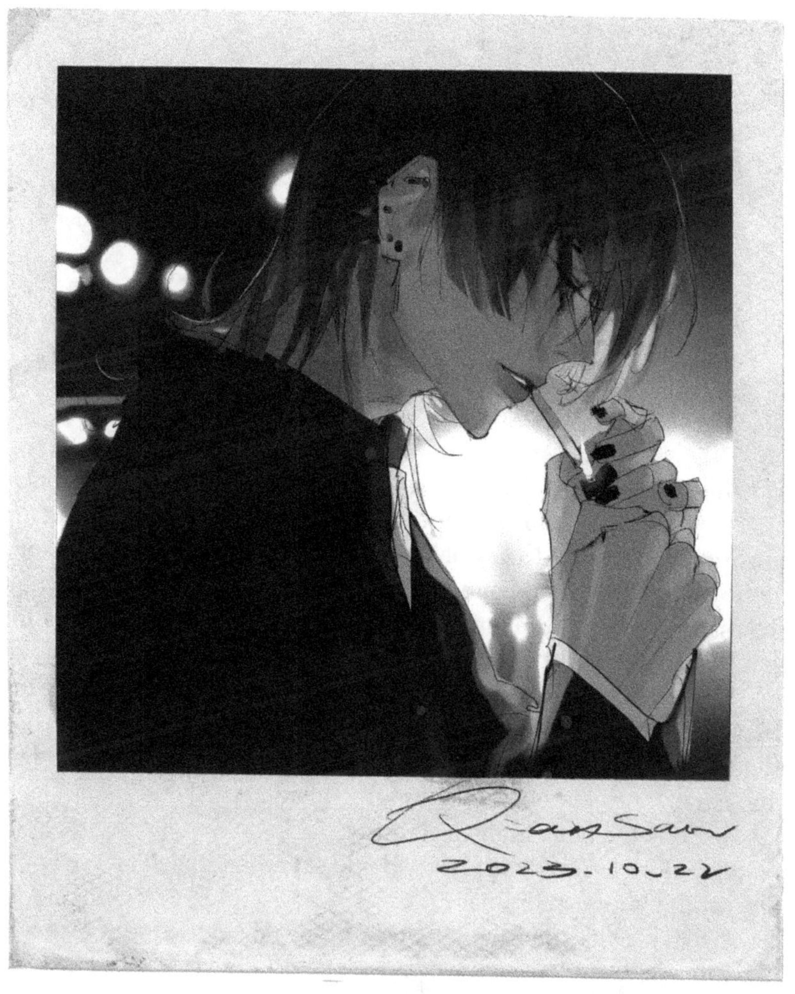

HUIYIN LIN

'My original character's storytelling.'

VOLUNTEERA

JOSHUA CICCONE

It was just as she had been told. She found the book on the very last street she looked down, under a cardboard box that was wet from the rain. It was tucked away behind a bush in a tiny grove next to some of the houses. It seemed only insects and small birds used it, because she did not see anything man-made, no boot prints or anything like that. There was only the cardboard and the book.

The book was a tightly bound thing, with two lengths of string that tied it closed in a bow. It was made of leather. The cardboard box that it had been under was falling apart, and it smelled like mildew and earth. She could not tell how long it had been there.

She took the book home.

She set it on the edge of her bed and sat cross-legged on the floor. She sat there for some time.

The string that tied the book rustled from some breeze through the unlatched window.

Suddenly, she burst to her feet and rushed around the house. She cleaned and made dinner and rearranged all the books on her bookshelf. She did all this without once looking at the book.

There was a moment where she took out her phone and looked at a picture of her mother for some time.

It was seven o'clock the next morning when she took the book, and she flew down the street. She ran fast enough to change the direction of the branches of bushes she passed. She took the bus that went all the way past the suburbs and the industrial estate and parks until it stopped on the high street. She stepped off the bus and flew towards the river.

There was a bridge next to the high street, and a host of stone-walled rooms that were blocked off from the public underneath. It was meant to be used as a club, but that had never happened, so the stone-walled rooms lay empty. She took out a key and ducked through the door into a stone hallway. She hurried to the furthest room from the door, flicking on a trembling electric light.

The book was still in her hand.

She walked to the centre of the room and undid the bow to open the book.

You would not have been able to guess, from looking at the cover, what was inside. It seemed to unhinge itself, like the jaw of some monstrous creature, and what was once something that you could probably buy at a shop became a leather tome older than time. The cover crackled and flexed. It expanded and morphed until it was like the skin of an old man: rough and wrinkled. The pages rustled like leaves as they moved and opened wider. It seemed that no one page was the same size, or even colour. Some were yellow, some had been browned to an extreme. The whole thing was aged in every way possible.

There was a short moment where she hesitated, eyes darting around, breath catching in her throat. She found herself murmuring, like there was an animal inside of her trying to get out.

She opened the book, and it breathed itself to life.

There was a slow *whoomph* sound as she placed the book on the floor. She turned to a page near the middle, stood properly to her feet, and took a deep breath. And then she chanted.

There was an instant change in the air. The wind outside picked up, and it came through under the door. It thrummed over the floor and rustled the mismatched pages of the large leather book. It wasn't just the wind that picked up. The temperature in the room rose until the place felt hot enough to burn – to burn skin and muscle.

That heat stopped her chanting and slammed her right down on the floor.

The book burst into flames. She scrambled away, hands clawing against the floor. The flames that came from the book were not red or orange or even blue. They were white hot and made the pages of the book bubble and spit. The lack of colour made the red hand that burst through the pages even more striking.

Then an arm, shoulder, torso and head appeared. Legs, knees, feet and a tall maroon creature heaved himself through the pages and onto the floor.

He was tall enough that his horns, black and curled, scraped slightly against the high ceiling. They stood about three centimetres on top of his head. His skin was a deep, deep red, as deep as maroon as dried blood. Veins curled all around him, and you could almost see deep, black blood pumping through them. There was a smell to him that reminded her of a bonfire on a quiet night. The kind of smell that is too strong and climbs into your lungs and sits.

The devil took a breath. He looked around and smiled. 'Who has summoned me?'

The fear was so acute, she could not open her mouth. It was a fear that came from her heart. Her chest. Her whole body falling into a catatonic state, slacking her jaw and her eyebrows as if she was having a stroke.

The devil had very large teeth when he smiled.

'There is no need to be afraid,' he said.

And, somehow, she relaxed and got to her feet.

'I need something from you,' she said.

'Most do.' His fingernails were very long, and they *tap-tap-tapped* against his leg as he drummed his fingers against it. 'It is not without price.'

She nodded. 'What should I give you in return?'

'It depends on what you need.' That smile, it was still there, sharp and red and monstrous.

She looked around, running a hand through her hair and shuffling her feet. 'It's a bit... awkward. I'm not sure if–'

'–It's alright,' the devil said. He had quite a bass to his voice. 'I'll make sure no... prying eyes can hear.'

She opened her mouth. 'My mother...' And that's when the tears came, hot and fast and stretching her into sobs that shook her shoulders and chest. She became hunched in her agony. 'She – I can't. I can't.'

The devil nodded. 'She is going to die.'

She could only nod.

'And you want me to...'

Her reply was only a whisper. 'I want her to be better. I want her back.'

'That's quite the ask.'

She could not look him in the eye.

'Are you sure?'

She nodded.

'Well... I'm sure you can guess what I want.'

And the devil outstretched his hand and waggled his fingers in a *'give it here'* sort of motion. His black fingernails shimmered in the light. His eyes were pure dark. Not black, not really, more of an innate nothingness.

'Oh...'

'If you don't think you can do it...' He pointed to the book.

'No! No.'

She took a deep breath.

'It's okay.'

She reached into her chest. The skin split easily, too easily. The devil watched hungrily as her fingers went through muscle and bone and lung. As her wrist flexed as she searched for what she wanted.

The heart came out quite smoothly. She passed it to the devil with trembling fingers, staring at the fleshy thing. The devil smiled wider when he took it in his hand.

He took a little bow. 'Thank you.'

And then he stepped back into the pages of the book, and with a sound as loud as thunder, he was gone.

Her eyes were unfocused as she gathered the fabric of her coat together and buttoned it up. She looked around for a moment and then walked out of the stone room underneath the bridge.

She took the bus home. The book rustled slightly in the cool air under the bridge.

The next day, she phoned her mother on her landline. Their conversation was short and littered with strange pauses, as her mind filled with this fog and her chest started to ache. It was her mother who put the phone down in the end, and she just stood there in her kitchen, staring at the floor and the wall and breathing slowly.

BOYS WILL BE BOYS

SHANAYE NICOLE PEACOCK

No one will believe the words from a woman's mouth. We lie and cheat and scheme. We submit to men even when we say our vows. Men double guess us and demote our self-esteem. I know I'm correct, why must you make me re-think? I can yell out the truth, I'll pour my drink, please, and down the misogyny like juice.

Because I'm just a female, I should shut up. I'm sorry I misunderstood. But we birthed your sex and raised you into your manhood. We didn't teach you to lack respect and act out when things get bad. That must have fallen from the tree that had been planted by your dad. Most of your life, you listened to your mother. But when another woman announces an opinion, your ears never seem to bother.

Care for women how you expect them to care for your child. Precious, and intensive, born with a heartbeat and a beaming smile. When it's a baby girl, you shiver; you know how men will treat her in this world. But that comes from you, your own gender and your own views. On how little women are needed on the planet that birthed you. Don't tell your girl not to wear this or not to go out this late, but allow your boy to banter and grope girls with their mates. You can't raise one to be neglected and have a caution towards men and raise the other to be the perv that apparently, you're saving from them. It's not the girl's fault old men glance and catcall as they walk down the street. You can't stop them from living. But you can teach boys to not cross boundaries when they come into heat.

Rarely do you see women act out from boys' shoulders and rejection.

'It's hard to see. Let me put on my glasses.'

'How the hell do you have an erection?'

That's right, instead of getting to know a woman and creating a safe place to make love. Your patience is too short. Skip the getting-to-know, whip out your phone and google the Hub. Couple of minutes of pleasure and degrading the women on your screen... Did you know she probably never wanted to be there? You came to the women that were forced by men to perform for a scene. Women like the dates and the romance and the leading up to the act. Men see it as a challenge; why aren't you more intact? With our feelings and our oppression... Society you say is damaged by prejudice and sexism. But it's not the man's fault you're trying your best. But when we say, 'me too', the truth is so hard for you to digest.

Get back to your room and grip the thing that makes women scared to move. And stroke your ego to the tits, then tell your girlfriend 'I don't approve'. Because if we post a photo with too much skin,

'That's gross don't you respect me.' But you get pleasure from someone else, that you cover up for none to see. Don't get stroppy and angry when men show interest and compliment me. When the day before you did what makes you feel sick when you think of men doing it to me.

You see, it's always the women who get blamed for relationships ending. Apparently, we're too rash and controlling over things you need to start mending. We react to your actions, so for once, maybe you could think twice. Because for years we watched our brothers do whatever they wanted and, for some reason, we needed to pay the price. I'm not changing what I find disrespectful. If you assume I'm a psycho, I'll give you the psycho in full. Because me and every other woman on this earth are fucking fed up with men and their entitlement for the gender, we fucking birthed. Don't get fucking disgusted when I wear a short top and a skirt. But when I'm not looking, you glance and start thinking about how hard you'll fuck her. The girl with her tits out, her arse hanging, and her teeny tiny waist. Sometimes when you fuck me, you close your eyes and picture another face.

If you want to find pleasure in a fake moan from your phone, I'll fucking pack your bags and you can fuck off all the way home. Because I'm here to give you what you want, a shoulder to cry on and an empathetic voice. But you'll risk that for a quick tug.

Because when men are horny, they're horny.

You know, 'Boys will be boys.'

That's okay, I'll let it slide. You know I can't take pictures in case men get the wrong idea. When you do the same fucking thing that keeps you up at night in fear.

'Girls will be girls.'

Determined and approachable. Oh, sorry, I mean, submissive and disposable. Again, I'm sorry, I apologise, I made a mistake. I'll do what you tell me, and you do the exact opposite of the boundaries that I state. I'll bite my tongue again and again. I'll keep living in a world that is run by the exceptional gender that we must call men.

APHRODISIA

SOFIA CAMARA-MARTINS

Pygmalion carved the waves of the
    sea across a woman's hips.
        Ships sailed, navigating the waters of
her ivory lips — mariners favoured the passive
                ones.

A crone offers the blood of
        a hawk for Aphrodisia.
A hawk, not a dove — a *bird* all the same.
The creature shrieked and struggled in her grasp, feathers
plucked, song silenced by
        the chisel that prodded and
        carved away the excess.
Freedom, chanted the crone, *is a construct.*

Freedom does not exist for
        Eros erects a prison and
        Aphrodite will not shackle the foul.

In Attica no man shall have his wishes granted.

Pygmalion kneels at the feet
        of love, of beauty
                of Aphrodite.
He prays but leashes his desires — conceals them
behind a white veil.
He replaced the hawk, gave
        purity for Aphrodisia.

A dove, not a hawk — a *sacrifice* all the
same. The creature sat gentle in his palms,
feathers stained, song silenced by
            prayer, his prayer sung in yearning.

Deities favour the passive ones, those
whose hearts are pierced by their
dulcinea.

In Attica, some men have their wishes
granted,
In Attica, Pygmalion is granted his Galatea.

A MEDIOCRE 'WIZARD'
AND THE ODD SHOP ON THE CORNER

JOJO CONNORS

The city of Muron was not a particularly nice place, nor was it a particularly horrible place; it was just a place where people lived, and people traded. It merely flirted with the map of Xutol, not bold and bright as the shining city of Dolis, but not a place swallowed by land like the rural town of Glia. It was a simple place.

Tall structures loomed over the cobbled roads that spread like veins across the city, casting shadows that consumed the alleys. In one such alley, off the main street and to the left of Kador Strumpet's Magic Emporium (which sold questionable potions for the layman traveller) a hunched over figure muttered to himself absentmindedly.

The figure looked to be a middle-aged man with a rather large dollop of unhinged madness mixed in and an even larger spoonful of greying hair and growing wrinkles on top of that. His fashion sense would best be described as confusing; he had two capes draped over him, but not in a cosy way, more in a way that made it seem like he put on a cape and then got attacked by a second. He wore purple boots that had been so weathered down that you could see the bottom of his heel out of the back of one of them. His trousers seemed to be poorly sewn together squares from years of fixing them, but poorly.

It was hard to say if he had a shirt or if it was just leftover fabric from fixing the trousers that he draped over his torso. Finally, he wore a sad wizard hat that slumped to the side as if trying to escape the fate that it had been sealed to.

He seemed to have lost himself in the cracks of the paving stones, staring at them with great determination as if the secrets to the universe were contained in the grit attempting to hold them together. The only thing that eventually broke his focus was the sweet jingle of the bell above the door of Kador Strumpet's Magic Emporium. A large cracking sound bounced off the walls of the alley as he straightened his back, making him grumble with annoyance as he walked towards the emporium's entrance.

Kador Strumpet was an odd man. He was around 4'1", a descendant of the Iron Dwarfs in the north of Rumone, but although the height stuck as his genetics were put through many different human relationships, he did not get the features of one. So, he just looked like a small boy, despite being sixty-four. His shop was a safety hazard, to say the least. He sold potions, as mentioned before, but he also sold ingredients, reanimation spells, ancient artefacts that may or may not curse you, and novelty keychains. The space also was not built for anyone over 5'7".

'What have I told you about entering this establishment, Lucius?' A squeaky voice came from behind the counter as Kador stared daggers (or in his magical way, pure negative energy) towards the towering, and again horribly dressed, man who barged through the front door.

The large man grumbled, expecting Kador to decipher his low-toned dialect.

Kador hopped up on what, at first glance, could be considered a chair, but was instead a vast range of metal pipe work that vaguely resembled a chair and only somewhat functioned as a chair.

Lucius had been distracted by a book that seemed to breathe.

'What is it?' Kador questioned reluctantly. After all, money is money, no matter who it's from.

'Need a new staff,' Lucius said, still mesmerised by the book that he could swear had now shifted slightly. 'What happened to the old one?' The shorter man arched an eyebrow, already knowing the answer, because it's always the same answer.

'It broke...' Kador lifted his hand to gesture Lucius to continue, 'I broke it'.

Kador sighed, then nodded. Then he jumped down from his culmination of pipes and walked into the back.

Lucius waited, glaring at the book that had now seemly grown legs.

The small shop owner returned with a staff made of an old tree branch and around six various coloured string knots, holding it together and standing at twice the height of him; not that this was an impressive fact.

Lucius grabbed it, transforming it into a normal sized staff with his stature alone.

'Fifty coins,' Kador stated, struggling to position himself in the 'chair' in a distinguished manner before giving up and sitting with one leg under him and the other bent in a direction it shouldn't be.

'Fifty coins?!' Lucius exclaimed, looking at the short man with confusion, 'but last time it was thirty! And this staff is barely holding together – look!' He picked a bit of bark off and placed it on the shop counter to make a point.

'Well, if you stopped breaking them every other week, then I wouldn't have to put the price up! They're high in demand,' Kador explained through gritted teeth.

'It's not even professionally made,' Lucius argued. He waved the stick around.

Silence from the shopkeeper.

Lucius sighed.

Got his pouch out and put fifty coins on the counter.

OVERHEARD

WHILST WORKING A NINE-HOUR SHIFT, SATURDAY, 11PM

CONNI LAURA GROVES

Smile a bit more love, and another pint of *san migwell* while you're at it. This is why I love the pub, match on, drinks flowing – this is the absolute lap of a life mate. Just that new girl, she's a proper sort, in't she? Not the kind of girl you'd settle down with, but if I were a younger man, I'd have 'er right here on my lap. Did you hear that, sweetheart? Oh, don't look so frightened, love, it was only a joke. What am I that ugly to you? That revolting? Can't even look me in the fucking eye when I'm talking to you. This is what I hate about this younger generation, all woke and feminist. All this MeToo bullshit. All these girls crying rape when they're just *dying* for it, like I love Russell Brand but suddenly it ain't politically correct to say that now. A bunch of attention seekers *wishing* they had someone interested, *wishing* someone would fuck them. *Dying* for it, mate. In't you love? **You're dying for it.** Oh, stop it now. It's just a little joke.

ONE LAST SONG OF HOPE

SONATA NEZNAMY

How strange when love picks up our bones
then rattles them to graves,
decorated in pale lilies and the scars of our dances.
That when our blooms do wilt,
our roots left there to dry
and new and bright flowers rest on the sill.

How fast the heartbeat quickens both in life
and before death.

One last song of hope.

TILL DEATH

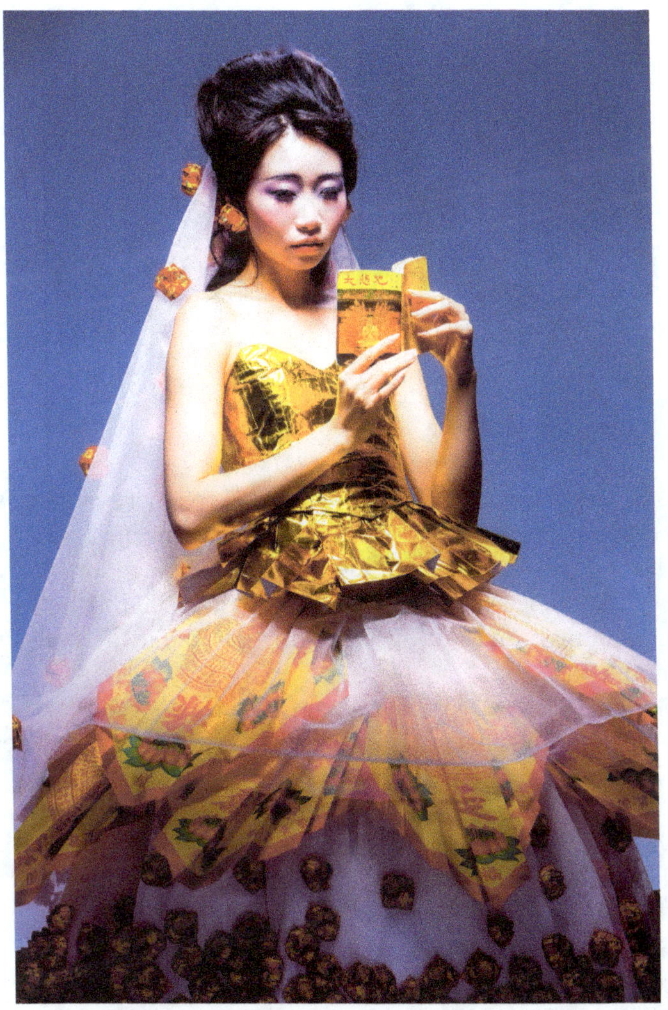

SYLVIA LIU

'Till death... reunite us again...', my imagination of the afterlife with a hopeless romantic twist.'

CAN'T BE TOO SAFE

ALEX MCALPINE

'It's me. It's Tom,' said the stranger on the security camera feed. 'It works—the program works. You have to let me in.'

The desk was cold against my forearms. I leaned forward on my clasped hands. The airlock was the only thing standing between the unfamiliar man and our—well, mine and Tom's, the real Tom's—magnum opus.

I tapped the centre of my glasses. The facial recognition hadn't found a match in my contacts or the interface, for the pointed jaw standing in the centre of the camera frame. That...was odd.

'C'mon Frankie,' he spread his arms out behind the screen, 'we've known each other for a decade. Stop messing with me.'

The man in front of me was average height, thin, and had short hair. Facial recognition couldn't find a match for his face on any computer database on the planet, which meant he could be right. The program could work.

Or he was an intruder trying to steal my research.

He wouldn't be the first.

'Frankie.' His arms dangled, his right thumb methodically cracking each of his fingers. 'Don't tell me you can't recognise me without interface glasses. You're better than that.' The playful smirk dribbled down his chin. I continued to frown, un-answering.

Tom's face only ever appeared behind a scrolling list of accomplishments. Each and every time I'd looked at him, my glasses reminded me he'd been valedictorian, the youngest recipient of the Innovation in AI award, the face of 'Science Today' and leader of my research team.

Humans didn't need to remember faces. So I never bothered to remember Tom's. Brown hair, taller than me. His face, like every other person I'd ever met, was startlingly boring, average, with no discernible characteristics.

Paint chipped at the edge of the intercom button as my finger ran over it. 'You don't have your ID,' I said through the camera monitoring the outside of the lab.

'It's in my office. Anyway, wouldn't matter if I did have it. The program worked. The building sensors don't have my biometrics anymore. I couldn't get through with my ID.' He placed a hand on the wall of the building, leaning into the camera. 'What am I saying? You know how the program design works.'

I reached into my pocket and pulled out a caffeine patch. The crinkling paper mixed with the buzzing sound of the computer monitors. The edge of the patch lined seamlessly next to the other four on my forearm.

'Where did we go for dinner when our funding was approved?' I asked.

He crossed his arms and smiled. 'East wind. You got a Bhan Mi. Against my recommendation.'

I pulled a hangnail off with my teeth. Had I posted a photo of our dinner on socials? A search appeared, scrolling inside my glasses.

'You're testing me? That's fine. But I wonder if you can describe my face without help from the interface?' He wiggled his eyebrows up at me through the camera. 'I thought you were smarter than that. The others,' he shrugged, 'they're mindless drones without AI help. But Frankie, you're brilliant. You're better than relying completely on interface glasses.'

My eyes narrowed at the black and white security footage. A bulleted list of achievements over someone's face was far more useful than noticing another set of teeth squished between two flaccid lips.

'Time for me to test you now. What colour are my eyes?' he asked. 'You can't cheat and find my photo online now. Was our last two decades of friendship a waste?'

The man on the security footage claiming to be Tom did not match the photo of last week's intruder on the 'Banned Wall.' Nor did he resemble the photo of the protesters who tried to burn down the lab. He also didn't look like the intern's boyfriend I'd found trying to download and steal my program two nights ago.

My program.

The one I'd spend the better part of five years designing. It was going to revolutionise personal data protection.

The search through socials running on my glasses came up with a photo of me standing alone in front of a sign reading 'East Wind', blue paint chipping off the side of the building. Tom wasn't tagged. Did I forget to tag him? He took the photo. If he'd triggered the program to protect his personal data, every trace of him would be deleted off the interface and every computer databank in the world, which included tags on social media.

Was it worth risking the security of a multi-million-dollar research program against a social media post I may or may not have forgotten to tag two years ago?

I took off my glasses.

I stared at the man until my eyes watered.

The skin on his squished nose was peeling. I had never looked at Tom without my glasses. I couldn't remember if I'd ever looked at anyone without interface glasses.

'Brown. The same shade as warm toffee. You have brown eyes that crinkle too much at the corners when you laugh.'

My palm slapped the large red button, unlocking the door to the airlock. A full set of bright teeth flashed in the security footage.

'Geez, Frankie, you scared me.'

Inside the airlock, he placed a hand on the window shielding the camera room. Over his right thumb was a scar from when he slipped cutting an avocado our sophomore year of uni. We'd sat in a hospital waiting room for an hour.

My eyes travelled up a sunburnt arm to his face. My fingers slid from the red button to a blue button covered with a plastic case.

'Frankie.' His muffled voice held a warning. 'What are you doing?'

My stare continued, unflinching. Without the shield of my glasses, I felt naked. A wall of text always buffered me from any direct connection with another human. 'My job is lab safety. You don't have an ID.' My index finger flicked open the plastic cover.

'Be reasonable,' he said. 'I get the funding. You write the program. That was the deal. We're partners.'

And yet it was his photo splashed across the cover of Computer Works Today magazine. Funny how, as a team, his name was always printed above everyone else's. He was always addressed as the lead researcher in press conferences.

My finger pressed the button half a centimetre before the first alarm sounded.

A red flash stole the smile from Tom's face. His hand slid down the window, leaving a smudge. His lips formed the word 'no,' but he never quite pushed out enough air to make a sound. His knees fell as a hazy yellow gas filled the airlock. Protecting the entrance to my lab. His shoulders landed with a thud on the floor.

The unconscious man in the airlock room twitched. I heard security slam open the stairway door. They'd be here in less than a minute. I fitted the interface glasses back to my face. The smudge on the airlock glass would need to be cleaned.

I opened the lab group chat and typed:

'Due to personal reasons, Tom is taking a leave of absence. I am taking over as team lead. On another note, an intruder was caught trying to break in this evening...'

MAP OF EMOTION

CHIA-YING LIN

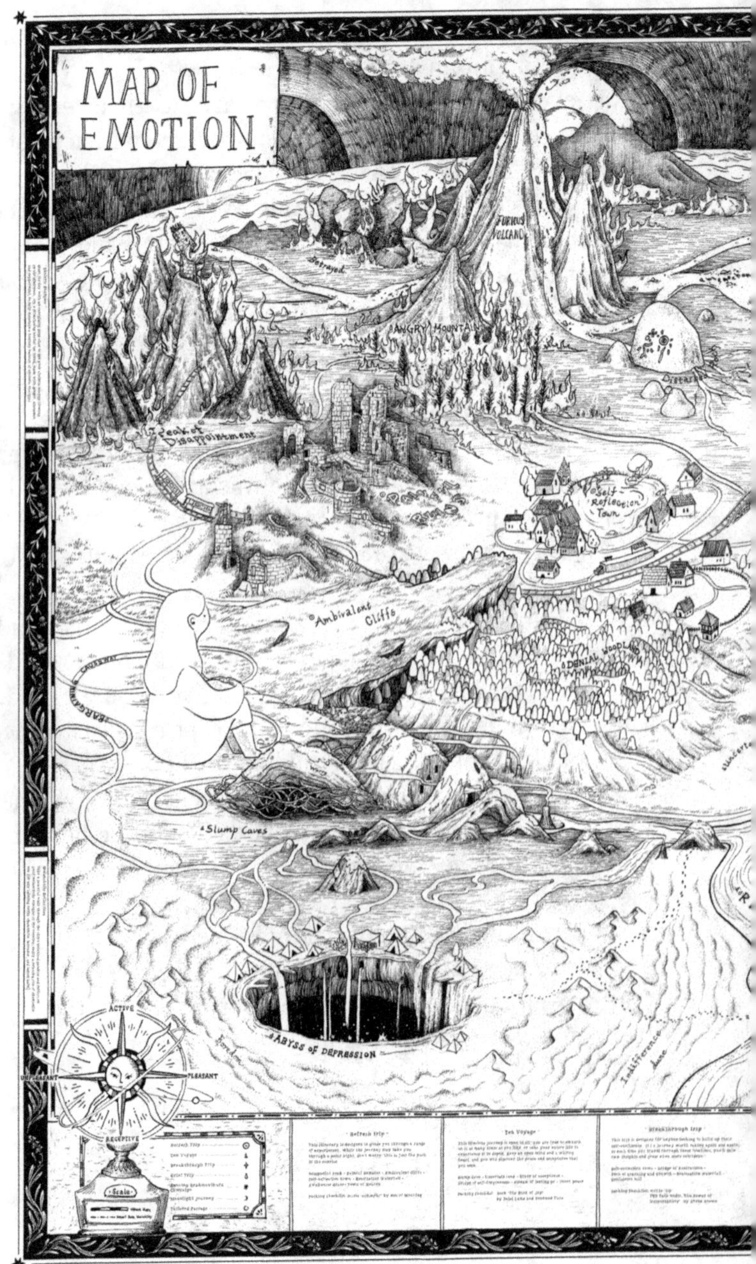

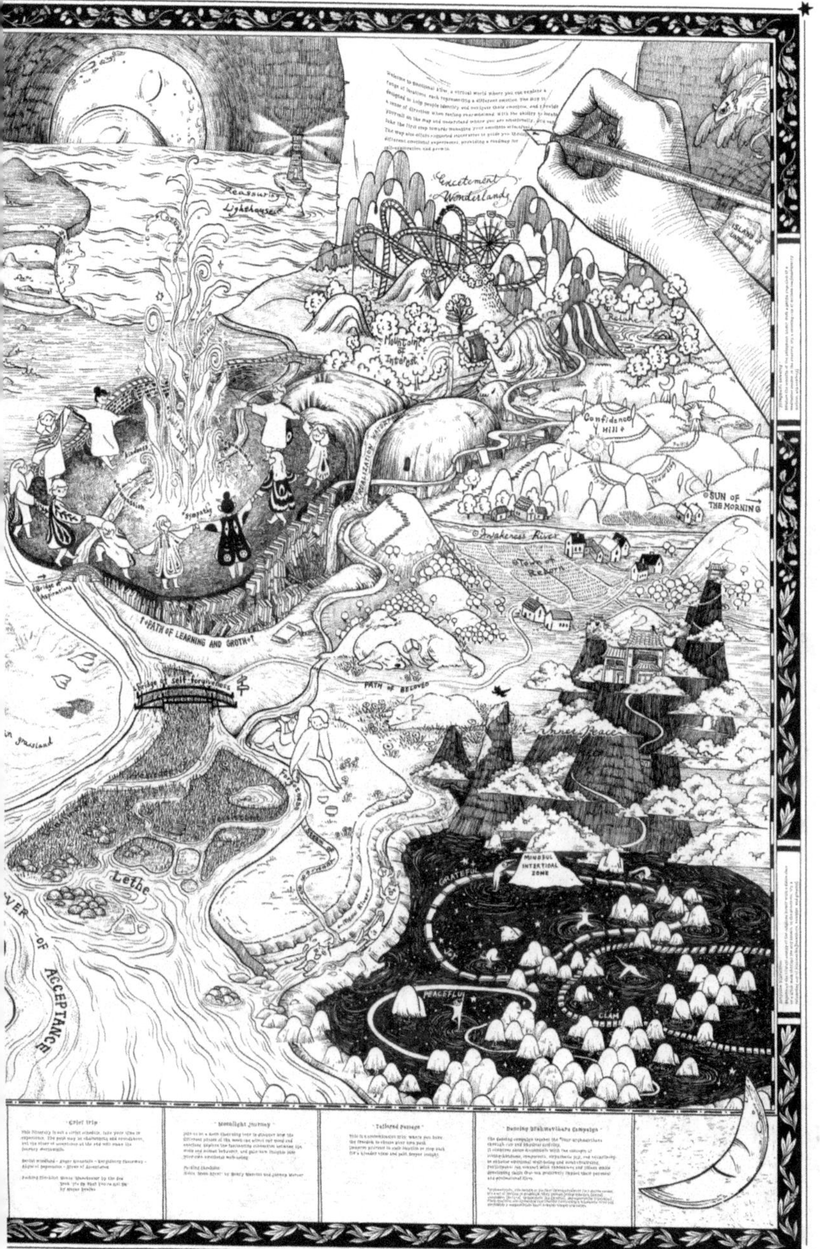

'I hope there's a map to navigate and recognize those complex and delicate emotions.'

CAN I BE ENOUGH?

SHANAYE NICOLE PEACOCK

Can I be enough? Can I ever be enough?
As much as they want, whatever they require, will that ever be me?
I'm just a girl... I love things like any other would and crave things anyone should.
Love. That grinding your teeth, wiping your tears and gripping your gut.
Love.

When I was a little girl, my parents constantly told me I was their princess and one day I'll find my prince, that I'd have to kiss a million ugly frogs to find the one.
Kissing ugly frogs was an understatement.
Kissing wasn't all I needed to do to find the one.
I had to rip my own heart out and leave it on the dirty floor.
Watch it get trampled on and mangled, watch it get cared for and thrown and having to de-tangle it, hold it myself and ask of them, can you handle it?

No. No, I can't.
Okay. I replace it. Rephrase it. Please.
I'll try harder to get the things people don't ask for.
I'll try harder to convince myself that you love me.
I'll try harder to be worthy of you just being nice.
So, please.
You can't hurt me anymore than you already have.
Crush me deeper into the ground, I've already sunk, I can't sink any further, I've swum to shore and tried to undo any damage you've done.
But I'd rather stink of desperation than be empty of love.

I'm a crumbled-up bit of tissue that you've coughed and sneezed into, tossed to the side.
That no one can be bothered to pick up, and I'm sorry I'm the only tissue in sight.
I'm the only one you can reach to clean yourself with, and I'm sorry I have holes and my edges are torn.
But I seem to do the job when you need it.

I'm sorry you can't buy more, and I'm sorry I can't replenish.
But I'm so stuck in that corner of your room that even if I tried to move, even just a little,
I'll tear completely.
Can I be enough?
Can I be enough for you?

SPEED OF LIGHT

JULES PENDRAGON

I wish I could go back in time.

That was probably something people wished for at least once or twice in their life. This was not the case for Jamie and Megan Brooks. Quite the contrary. The twin siblings did not want to have that burden. But ignoring the world around them was not so simple. They lived with it while keeping up with their normal life. They tried their best to remain as mundane as possible.

'Mr Brooks, are you paying attention?' a voice called out to Jamie.

He looked up from his notes to the teacher. His pen had remained on the same page, writing nothing else. He had spaced out again.

'Yes, Mr Sheffield,' he replied, picking on his jeans to focus on something else rather than his gaze. He was embarrassed enough.

The class was no bigger than thirty freshmen. All of them turned back to look at the board once the professor resumed his lesson. Zoning out was not the optimal thing to do with the upcoming finals. But what did he care? He was considering dropping out; his head was in the clouds during class. His mockups never lived up to the professors' expectations. He could feel himself drifting into another daydream despite the luminous light coming through the window. He jerked himself awake with a stab to the hand with his blue pen, a habit he picked up from the nerdiest in the class. The professor was highlighting the key points of brutalist architecture in the 50s when the door suddenly opened.

'Um, excuse me, professor. I need to borrow Jamie for a few moments,' the feminine version of himself peeked inside the classroom.

Mr Sheffield stopped pointing at the board and turned towards the intruder. 'Why? Is it urgent?'

'It is...' she replied, picking on her cream sweater. 'Our dog is in the vet, and they called wanting to sacrif–'

'Oh, dear,' the professor interrupted her and shook his head. 'Right, yes. He can go.' 'Thank you,' Megan said.

Jamie left the room as quietly as possible with the most neutral expression he could muster. He shut the door softly behind him.

'We don't have a dog,' Jamie said once they were beyond reach.

'Yea, I know.' Megan rolled her eyes, pulling out a letter from the half-moon bag strapped across her shoulders. 'We've got a new one.'

'Crap,' the eldest brother blurted out, looking at it.

08/06/13
Prevent the car accident at Cornwall St.
12:56

It had taken a while to determine that the numbers at the top meant the month, day and year. At least today's instructions were clear. Jamie took a glance at his watch. It was ten to twelve. Couldn't she have got here faster?

'We gotta run,' Jamie grunted, taking longer steps. Megan sprinted a little to keep up with his steps. Her heels were making it quite difficult. 'Why do you keep wearing those things?'

''Cause I bought 'em, and I like 'em,' she panted.

They reached the stairs of the university and turned east. A handful of people were passing by the street. Jamie wanted coffee but didn't think he had enough time to buy any. It was no surprise to the siblings that it was already drizzling. Megan muttered a low curse and attempted to cover her dirty blonde hair with her arm. The brother pulled up his hoodie. They succeeded in turning on the street when a bolt of lightning struck.

The rain suddenly stopped. On the street, the pedestrians froze and faded away. A cat slunk backwards around a corner. He held onto Megan's hand. Around him, the world turned black and silent.

A moment later, Jamie became aware of the sound of his breathing. Their surroundings were different and yet the same. Instead of grey noon light, the sky blazed with blue tones. Jamie swiftly pulled out his phone from his jean pocket and tapped his screen twice. It was 6 August 2013. 12:55. They successfully travelled nine years back in time.

'Come on!' Megan tapped Jamie's shoulder before rushing to the crosswalk of Cornwall St. A woman was crossing, looking at her phone screen, too busy to notice she was walking in red.

Jamie chased after his sister. As he was faster, he ran past her and ahead to get to the lady as soon as possible.

'Ma'am!' Megan cried out, trying to gain the woman's attention, but to no avail. She was wearing headphones.

Jamie grabbed the woman's arm once he reached the crosswalk and pulled her back. The lady yelled in protest. Maybe she thought they were about to rob her. His grip was firm enough to lead them three steps back.

'Excuse—' the woman shrilled. 'Let me—'

'Ma'am,' Jamie interrupted, patiently. 'You were on red.'

'What?' she took off her headphones.

Jamie did not have time to utter another word as a dark blue coupe swerved towards the street corner, way above the speed limit, and dashed through Cornwall. Megan's gaze was focused on the car, then she glanced at her watch. *12:56*. There were no sounds of a crash. Good, that was it.

The lady looked at the car and then back at Jamie, dumbfounded.

She must have realised that, had the young man not pulled her back, the car would have crashed her to bits.

'Please, be more careful,' he shrugged, as if their encounter was merely a coincidence. Megan nodded slowly and headed back south towards the university. Jamie jogged until he reached her.

'So, who was that?' Jamie glanced back at the lady, who, this time, was walking to the other side of the street. He then took the time to survey her formal attire.

'Am I a fortune teller too?' Megan let out a sigh. 'If only the Messengers spilled the beans.'

'Right,' he grumbled.

Travelling was a closed cycle. So, when they turned to the corner, a lightning bolt struck once more. A bird flew backwards. Around them, the world turned black and silent. A moment later, they were back in 2022. Rain replaced the sunny sky. The pedestrians reappeared on the sidewalk. One bumped into Jamie; a letter fell off the stranger's coat.

'Hey, wait up!' Jamie called out.

But the stranger kept walking, losing himself in the crowd. Megan let out a sigh.

'Let him be,' she picked up the letter. 'Whoever he is, he won't answer our questions. We tried that, remember?'

'Yea...' he conceded and looked at the paper in his sister's hand.

Susan Levine

'That should be our lady,' she mumbled, pulling out her phone to google the name. Jamie peeked over her shoulder. As she scrolled through the links, they read that the very Susan Levine, the pictures proving it was the woman they had saved, was appointed by the town's new mayor.

'Great, we're saving politicians' lives now?' Jamie complained. 'So much for travelling for the common good.'

THORN IN YOUR SIDE

JULES SHIPTON

no part of me
can you steal
this raging spirit of El Niño
wallops your lust to dominate
land people and sea
you see
you cannot tame me
no part of me can you disguise
dust layers, my voice
as I roar thunder with might
across their history
you see
no one can touch me
my courage of defiance
my solo heart
vanishing in daylight
ghost dancing
jesting war cries
painted skin, bare back, hair streaming
coyote baying toward smoky halos
at the western gate dawning
ageless blights upon this land
no one can invent Me
mammoth sculpture reigned in rock
painted skin, bare back, hair streaming
I am invisible
I fly, I fly, my bones do not lie
no sign to pass me by
golden eagle
I was born to die
a thorn in your side

WINDY CITY

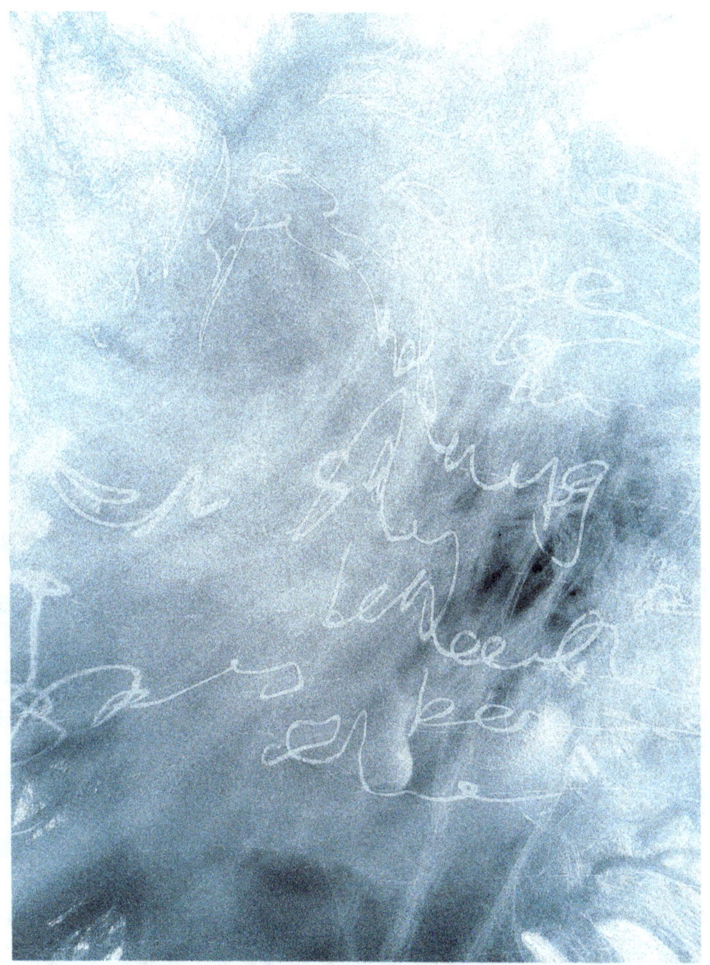

IMOGEN CROCKFORD

'I was inspired by experimental portraiture and pieces that capture motion and integrate written text into a photograph.'

SAGE GREEN
IS THE CALMEST COLOUR

JULIA COLOMBO

Sage green is the calmest colour.

It's the colour of the forest surrounding my house on a hazy summer morning before the air's got too unbearable.

It's the colour fawns hide in before they've learned to defend themselves; before they've learned, they *need* to defend themselves.

It's the colour of one wall in every room of my high school, which was my middle school, which was my elementary school, which is one of the safest places I have ever known.

It's the colour I see when basil and oregano mix in the lemon juice and olive oil the chicken cooks in. It's the colour of the flecks on the white bread my mom dips into the mixture – 'This is how Great Grandpa used to do it' – she eats it without taking a breath.

It's the colour my brother will wear when he scours foreign lands for something safe, or something dangerous; the thought makes me want to hide him away, but I love my brother, so I love the colour he, too, has decided will be his.

While I've decided sage green is, in fact, the calmest colour, the colour of nature and baby deer and security, it could be someone else's nightmare. It might be too close to the green of army fatigues for some, or remind them of people they love, people they hate, people they've lost, people they've hurt. It could remind you of your rapist's t-shirt or vomit or your mother's garden—a garden full of weeds and thorns and predators sucking the life out of anything beautiful that might have grown there once upon a time.

So, no, sage green is not the calmest colour.

How could my calmest colour be anyone else's?

FAR

SHANAYE NICOLE PEACOCK

A loud scream is heard, and a faded spotlight turns on. The four friends are huddled in the centre of the stage, looking down at a well, dressed in school uniform.

BRADLEY
He– he just fell.

GRACE
How– how, Ryan. Ryan how?!

Ryan is zoned out of the conversation.

BRADLEY
Should we just leave him down there? It was just us here, right?

GRACE
Yes, I hope it's just us.

BRADLEY
Might not have been. I don't want people to find out. Let's go.

TIFFANY
No, Bradley. **(Pause)** They'll ask questions.

All sharply look towards the audience.

GRACE
Ryan, tell them to close their eyes. Ryan!

RYAN
(To the audience) Just shut your eyes for one second.

TIFFANY
How did he fall? Grace, tell me now.

GRACE
It was all of us. All of us, don't stick it all on me.

TIFFANY
We need to fucking save him.

GRACE
We can't, we– we just can't, it's too far now.

TIFFANY
You want to just leave him down there? What's wrong with you?

RYAN
He deserved it. We all know that.

TIFFANY
How can you say that?

GRACE
Ryan's right, leave him to die.

BRADLEY
It doesn't feel right. He was our–

GRACE
Bradley, he was nothing to us. **(Grabs Tiffany's face)** Tiffany, listen to me, he was nothing.

TIFFANY
Get off me!

BRADLEY
If we're leaving, we've got to go now.

TIFFANY
No! No!

RYAN
Tiffany, we did it. Now we let it be.

TIFFANY
But everyone's going to–

RYAN
Grab your shit, let's go, come on, let's fucking go. Grace, hurry up.

All run off stage.
After a while, Tiffany enters centre stage and looks down the well where the man has fallen.
Tiffany sits down.

TIFFANY

Hey, I don't know if you can hear me, but I'm just going to speak, anyway. **(Pause)** And I want you to know you can speak to me too, if you're alive. Please say you're alive. I– we didn't mean to put you in this situation. We're just kids, you know? I'm sorry, we're all sorry. **(To audience)** Don't tell them I came back. I'm not allowed– we're not allowed to tell. I'd be told off; we'd all be told off. **(To hole)** Wouldn't we? I'd be in big trouble. **(Bangs head with hand. Takes deep breaths) (To hole)** Hello? Come on, I'm your girlfriend, you can't keep ignoring me. I love you so much. I miss you so much, why did you stop coming round my house for a while? I know climbing through my window was never great, but I've always found it romantic in films, and I could tell you enjoyed sneaking around, and you always brought over my favourite cake, carrot, I just miss that. Please come back up, try and come back up to me. You told me I was the only one for you. The only one you wanted to love and touch. And I want you back.

Tiffany exits the stage.
Bradley enters centre stage and looks down the well where the man has fallen.
Bradley paces the stage.

BRADLEY

Hello? Hello? You down there or what? I know you're probably not dead. You always try and find a way to come back. People are gonna find out. Find out you're down here. And you know what? Some part of me hopes they do, even though I know how people are gonna look at me when they find you. **(Look to audience)** Will you tell 'em? Huh? Tell 'em all who's down here? What we did? Everyone's got to know. It ain't right. **(To hole)** I fucking hate myself, hate myself because I want them to find you. Hate myself for what I did. I did it. I was the only one. You told me. You told me that. **(Long pause)** You helped me out so much. You helped me through my homework, even when my dad kicked me out of the house. You were the one who gave me a place to stay. My dad was, and still is, a fucking abusive dickhead, but I forgot all of that when I was at yours and– **(Long pause)** I could always count on you, for anything, any help at all. You don't deserve this **(Pause)** you do, but you don't. I don't fucking know. And I'm sorry. I'm sorry people are gonna find you soon.

Bradley exits the stage.
Grace enters centre stage and looks down the well where the man has fallen.
Grace is squatting/pacing.

GRACE

Why'd you do it? You jumped. You did this to yourself. I hope you're dead. I hope every fucking bone broke on the way down. **(To the audience)** Do you think it hurt? It's quite a long fall. **(Falling whistle and explosion)** Brain damage. Did anyone else come here? To visit him? Tiffany probably did. She's a wreck. **(To hole)** Because of you. **(Long pause)** Why her? Huh? Tiffany? I knew you were with her as well; I knew it wasn't just me. You saved my life, every day I was just downing drink after drink, forgetting every lesson at school, and because of you, I'm sober. I'm 5 months sober because you sat me down and told me to sort my shit out, and I did, and then I fell in love with you and you said you loved me back, you sick fucker. I hope you're dead down there because if there's even the slightest bit of life in you when they drag you out of here, I will beat you to fucking death, you cunt. **(Long pause) (Tremor)** You're a prick, you're an arsehole, you're an idiot, I just never thought you were a– I love you. I shouldn't, but I do. **(Gets up to leave)**.

Grace exits the stage.
Ryan enters the stage and looks down at the well where the man has fallen.
Ryan stands in complete spotlight.

RYAN

I don't even know why I'm here. I couldn't give you an answer. This has all messed me up. Do you know what's gonna happen to me if this comes out? If they find you? I'm not sorry. I can't be sorry. Remember that night after school, we stayed up for hours, chatting. You listened to me, more than anyone ever has. You brought me popcorn, and you told me Diet Coke tasted exactly the same as Dr Pepper, and I had to break the news to you that Dr Pepper is actually cherry flavoured and how you didn't know carrot cake had actual carrot in it. **(Laugh turns into a cry)** And the next week, you asked me to stay round, and you– you told me I could trust you. And then– and then. Fuck, I can't even say it. I came here to finally say it. Why am I still afraid of you? **(To audience)** No, that's what I said. No. **(To hole)** And you said it was fine because I didn't know any different. **(Long pause)** And now, everyone's gonna find out what you did to me. To all of us. The police, my parents, our mates. Who knows if there's anyone else. You did this. And Tiffany and Grace and Bradley blame themselves for ruining your life, but you did this to yourself. Why would you think this is all okay? **(Long pause)** You were our teacher, Mr Lenny, our teacher.

Ryan exits the stage. The light goes out.

THE END

LAKE FULL OF STARS

REBECCA CHANDLER

Oh, humanity,
your idiocy astounds me;
I adore your bright-eye
stupidity.
The way you try
to find stars in the surface
of a lake, and when they
slip, shimmer, shatter
into ripples beneath your fingers,
or under the breath of the wind,
you tip back your head and
lift up your feet, float in the
dark and stare up, and feel
as lost in the ethereal, stretching,
shadow-light glow
as if you'd always known you
couldn't touch the stars with
your bare hands.

But instead, as the lake whispers
a thousand seashell secrets
into your ears, something flies up
made of innocence and fear,
of quicksilver laughter,
of brushed away tears,
and flutters, moonlit moth,
lace-winged hope,
to gently brush against
the floating, flaming, firefly lights
that illuminate the water tonight,
that illuminate the sky of your eyes
until it feels almost that you've
swallowed the trailing, spiralling
dust of the stars,
woven it into your bones and
patterned with smoke and shadow,
turned ash, turned dust.
There's both more and so much
less to us than when we first
thought the lake was full of stars.

I-90 TO I-10

NOAH CHANDLER

These are the new-neo-postwave-postmodern-contemporary
Americana youths,

who drive a dented Nissan through state lines and state parks,

who stop at gas stations to smoke and mourn the loss of a man they've
never met: Camel Joe.

who put on Lou Reed and Johnny Cash and sort of wish they could've
been like them,

But they know that the hardly hard work of sculpting this modern
Americana is done, wrapped up by Kerouac, Ginsburg and Hunter S.
eons ago.

If only they'd been there first to kick up the dust now settled on Route 66.

Now they stare at greasy roller dogs and curse the smoothed-out
country and wonder what it might've been like to spread a map on the
hood of their car and feel the heat on their palms while paper flapped
in the breeze.

What it might've been like to roll through
this land of dried earth and asphalt,

pulled forward by a shimmering heat at the end of the road,

while 1-800 numbers offered them their fate and refineries burned
through dusk.

FUJI, WITH YOU

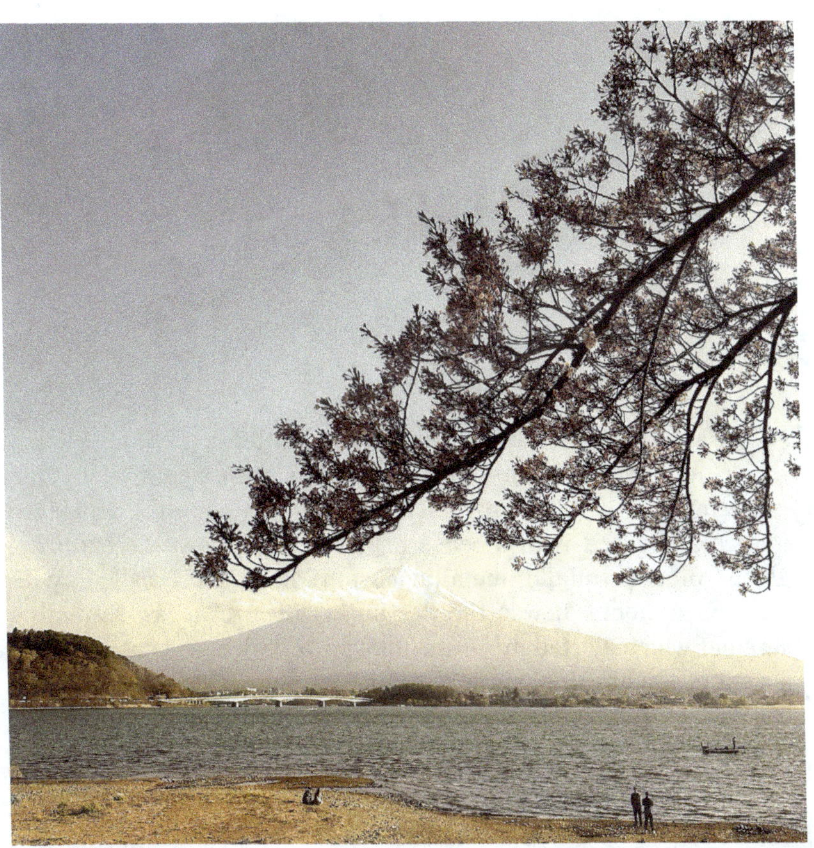

KARINA MIRIKLIS

'The simplicity of the snapshot reflects the importance of pausing to breathe and share meaningful moments with our loved ones.'

GLACIES

STEVE KENT

The arrival of the Obelisk complicated matters.

As my semi-conscious body, a crimson mass of tender, pulsating burns and oozing, blistering pulp, lay upon the depressed mattress, I gazed with a sense of heedless joy into the enduring gloom of the squalid metallic carton of which I called, with reluctance, home. It was the fleeting pacifism of a fast-retreating slumber which alerted me of the unexpected silence, a droll respite, absent of the howling winds which, since our arrival, had battered the eroding hull of the star galleon Elysian without once desisting from their ferocious wrath. I struggled to recall a similar furlough of this relentless tempest, manifested by a ceaseless, emphatic barrage which thundered across the vast barren tundra, as deluges of icicles shattered as they waltzed upon the Elysian's frail hull as it lay plagued by the infernal squalls. But now, I became fixated upon the preservation of a tranquil slumber and struggled to contemplate the existence of any newfound serenity. I rejoiced, for that morning, out of the countless that had preceded it, felt somewhat different.

It was during my conceited attempts to wrestle back reanimation that I first became aware of the presence of a bright protruding light, which crept across the emptiness of the chamber, manifesting an ethereal spear, shimmering as its alluring, gilded tip pierced the crisp air. After resisting its magnetism to preserve a few precious moments of slumber, I found its nourishing presence intruding upon my swollen eyelids, and without hesitation, I tugged my tattered blanket tighter before rolling away. But fending off the adamant rays, I soon discovered, was a futile endeavour. Defeated, the boiling photon devoured me amongst its warm, smothering glow. That was when I first felt a sharp, throbbing pain scurry along my exposed, seared flesh.

I awoke. In a sudden, dazzling flash, I was blinded, my bloodshot eyes set ablaze as they snapped open. I recoiled, burrowing my hands into the decayed mattress. I felt stunned. Or winded. It is difficult to remember. I rolled away, exposing the large amethyst blotch that stretched down the left side of my body as I gazed over the edge of the mattress into the darkness beneath the grated iron floor. A force of habit encouraged me to await the next rupture of steam escape from the decaying pipes which lay below. They were idle, not restless, awaiting the foul, bloated pulse of the Elysian to flow past before groaning back into position. I had yet to learn if the arduous murmurs were the Elysian showing its age or if, in fact, they were the muffled agonies of the Figurehead, a once mortal man, who hung crucified underneath the tip of the Elysian's bow. Long had I pondered if he felt the cold. When I last ventured outside to observe his lobotomised torment, a deluge of frost had begun to settle upon his grey, blemished flesh. How many glimmers of ancient, forgotten stars have departed within the emptiness of his vacant onyx eyes? But now his mouth lays forever dormant as the mists whirl within this void chamber. With each failing breath, his pulse summons life into the star galleon of ancient vessels through two tempered ducts protruding from his torso before the pipes once more fall slumber at the demise of each shallow exhale.

But that morning, I could not endure this spectacle. Instead, the light bore down upon me its simmering admiration, which prompted a terrific agony that ignited my face. I tore my palm from beside my cheek, catching between my numb fingers' fragments of scalded flesh, which melted away as if I were the finish of a repugnant candle. Dropping the feeble remnants to the floor, I watched as they decayed into a foul purple haze, evaporating into an alluring musk which hypnotised the brisk air. I bit my bloodied lip, coughing as I ascended from the pools of dried, rusty blood.

'Kai? Kai?' I called out in a dry, hoarse tone as I gasped for air. There was no answer, for he was already dead, buried alongside our brethren beneath a crisp blanket of shallow, unbroken snow. How could I forget? For it was Kai of whom we mourned last. So, I panted, alone. I summoned the strength to push myself upwards, but in my damaged and broken state, I fell. The impact of my body smashing against the floor pushed the air from my lungs. Winded, I lay beside a lump of molten flesh, absorbing the foul, succulent vapour of which I had become. It was in this moment of weakness that I recounted a blurred recollection that in my younger and more adventurous days, I would dash towards the window of my bedroom and absorb the radiance of a clear, blue sky. But that morning, once I had regained the ability to stand, a faint, frail wobble substituted any notion of an energetic jolt, and after I slipped on a pair of boots and fastened my torn jacket, I proceeded towards the porthole amidst the frigid atmosphere of the chamber.

The bleakness of the vicinity surrounding the Elysian amplified the direness of our situation. As the star galleon lay crippled, the enduring deluge continued to congregate against the shattered, charred hull. The horrid blizzard had been quick to engulf us within a dense layer of pale, gleaming snow. However hard we laboured, either shovelling or chipping away at the encasing slabs of ice with our rusted and warped pickaxes, by the next endeavour, the Elysian was closer to being entombed whole. On occasion, my numb ears would sustain the clashing of tools against the Elysian's hull, listening as a quartet of grunts and groans resonated from hunchbacked crewmen who toiled like a collection of crooked hobgoblins. The eroded spires which adorned the opposite portion of the Elysian, in comparison, towered upwards like a foul cluster of rugged iron steeples, their wicked tips piercing the dense layers of blackened clouds like sharp, rusted needles. In the absence of thunderous bells, a gentle euouae, a faint whistle or the melody of a soft lullaby, these stalagmites endured an endless assault of merciless gales that crashed against their form like a ram against the steadfast wall of an impregnable fortress. It was within a narrow crevasse between the Elysian and its steadfast anchor that one could listen to the glorious siege, lifting his head upwards, capture a pinch of the ebony sky hiding between the ceaseless fluttering remnants of an overhanging solar sail and surrender to the distant horns, calling forth rapid strikes of lightning that flashed across the din.

As I questioned how long I would be rewarded with an undisturbed observation of this expanse of malevolent pulchritude, a heavy burden began to brew within my ravenous stomach. Despite a cumbersome grin stretching across my scolded face, I took joy in the realisation that these precious moments eclipsed the putrid fallacy of our hallowing epoch. Did I now stand before the porthole as a relic of a bygone past, watching in silence as faint, distant spheres accelerated back into shadow? Would my sole company, one distant morning, be the unfamiliar glimmer of timid stars emerging across the empty sky, hovering as astute as a pack of vultures? It was these moments, knowing this tranquillity, this paradise, this grand oasis upon an unbroken world, was temporary, which red any sense of excitement or elation.

But I continued to glance across the immaculate canvas, which lay idle as a sandy beach absent of a calm morning tide, as millions of droplets of snow floated as bales of glistening cotton. In my ignorant excitement, the pains of daylight eluded me, as I held my palm before the glass, tracing my bloodied finger along the outline of the distant, snow-capped mountains, naïve of the growing scent of immolation. These distant mounds stood bundled together beneath an enormous central peak, a colossus that ascended towards the fading stratosphere. I could not decide upon the purpose of their symmetry. Were they ordered shoulder to shoulder or packed tight in formation? What, or who, had arranged them in this fashion? What were they guarding with their enduring vigilance? The summit of what I nicknamed Goliath, a balding apricot scalp absent of snow and ice, stood encompassed by a violently blackened gash, cascading an eruption of glimmering stars across the blackened cosmos. Had any mortal climbed them? Was I to become a curious Icarus, pondering inside his metal cage upon a fallacy of geographic hyperbole? Perhaps I would ascend that distant summit and lay there, watching as the stars collapse upon me. I chuckled as the porthole became masked by the purple hue.

Something made me feel alive once again.

THOU ART TO US
THE HEALING TREE

BIANCA FOGAH

When she had to leave her bougie $4,000 NYC apartment to go on a self-care retreat, she hadn't expected to get her hands this dirty. It's all a bit of fun, her mother had said after her last breakdown. The last of many. The brochure her mother shoved in her hands announced 'naturalistic' and 'cathartic'. Instead, she felt animalistic and bestial.

With her monthly call allowance, she called her mother.

'They have us building a raft to go out to sea, Mother! Something about how God will save us if we repent. We're pulling apart trees and breaking bones of live animals! It's barbaric!'

'Don't be ridiculous. The outdoors never hurt anyone, and killing is part of the human condition.' Her farm-raised mother told her.

'Please, you have to let me come home,' she pleaded.

'It will do wonders for you to truly live a hands-on life, Marisha. You've been gifted with a chance to cleanse yourself with the fruits of Mother Earth. Finish the course, then we can talk about the next steps.' Her mother hung up.

The group leader watched them make their raft.

Marisha stripped the trunk of its flesh and tied it down with veiny vines. She'd already mutilated its children to build the base and used its sticky sap to bind it, having murdered defenceless animals for their hides and baby bones—perfect for filling those small gaps. Together with the other sinners, she built the raft one body at a time. They told her in her orientation, 'It's nothing you wouldn't have wasted as part of your lavish lifestyle, buying frivolous things and on-the-go coffees with plastic containers.'

The man working beside her, his hands bloodied from the sap of scalped trees, started singing.

'Thou art the true and heav'nly Vine,
Our very source of life;
By Thee we live, in Thee abide,
And rest from all our strife.'

Over and over.

She wanted to cry. To beg the trees for forgiveness, for wisdom, for strength against adversity, but it was too late. When the raft was complete, she and the others gingerly pushed the raft into the water. Waves gently flowed over the raft as they all went out to sea.

As their fear grew, so did the sea's ferocity. Waves crashed against them. Without shelter, they started tipping overboard, one by one. Screams were overshadowed by an ancient rage. She had never truly believed in God, and thought this, perhaps, was her punishment.

It was just her and the man left. He started singing again.

'Thou art to us the healing Tree;
Our death Thou didst endure;
Thou on a tree for us wast slain,
That we may have Thy cure.'

She was grateful for the wave that took her. The fizzy bubbling tickled her eardrums. Salty water filled her nasal passages. The undercurrent dragged and ripped her across the ocean. She'd had enough of life months ago, and now she'd taken the lives of Mother Earth.

She felt a moment of relief, then everything went dark.

HEADLINES

BETTY WATERS

Living with the headlines
of me is easy.
The poetry, delightful;
It's the prose
that's harder, [1]

1 and the footnotes.

WILD BY NAME

RACHEL MATTHEWS

It started, as many stories often do, with a girl in the woods.

Or, more specifically, by a wishing well in the woods.

The only exception was the wishing well from which the town had pilfered its name. Rumours swirled around it. There were stories of children falling in, their remains never to be found. There were claims that the well often disappeared, only to reappear days later. There was a myth that an evil spirit lived at the bottom, waiting to steal lost souls.

Lydia Wild had never had any interest in the well before, she hadn't even seen it. When little George Riddley had heard this, he'd laughed at her, called her a coward and claimed she didn't have the courage to venture near it.

Lydia Wild was many things – but she was most definitely not a coward.

That very day after school, as the sky started to bleed red, Lydia cycled to the edge of town, abandoned her bike on the side of the road, and stepped inside the woods.

They were different from how she'd imagined. There were no monsters lurking behind tall, spindly trees and no wolves spying at her from between long, groping branches.

Instead, there was only the winter wind biting at her skin. The scent of grass and the soft orange hue of the sun brushing the woodland floor. There was only the sound of birds and the rustle of leaves. There were only the trees spread out around her, their branches open wide and their tops vanishing into the sky.

It struck her that she could climb up into the arms of a tree and disappear forever.

The woods were infinite as she navigated her way through them, her uniform snagging on bits of twigs as she made her way.

And then... there it was.

It was ancient and rotting. One side of its circle significantly taller than the other. The bucket that had been there once upon a time had long since gone.

Without hesitation, she peered into it. Local boys were known to shout rude words down into its dark. George Riddley had once claimed that he'd heard something shout back...

Lydia was entranced by it. By how deep the blackness was. How even as she stared into it, it felt as though the darkness was staring right back.

She gazed into the tunnel of the well, and she ached and realised that while she didn't want to fall in... she wanted to jump. To dive in and see if, like Alice, she would descend into another world.

It felt possible.

She was thirteen years old, anything seemed possible. Hands trembling, she dropped her rucksack to the ground and rummaged through it until her hand clasped around a tiny silver coin.

The woods grew silent – as though all the trees and critters had stilled to watch her. Suddenly, it occurred to her that she didn't want to waste her wish. That she couldn't allow it to be any flimsy, casual old thing.

So, Lydia Wild tilted her head back, closed her eyes and wished for everything.

She wished for everything that she hadn't experienced yet, everything she hadn't seen or felt. She wished for everything that she could ever be.

Everything.

Even then – small, and runty, and wearing a uniform that swamped her – Lydia felt as though her soul was too big for her body… her dreams too wild for such a narrow place.

She flipped the coin and watched as the tiny sliver of silver soared through the air before being swallowed by the well.

Then she waited.

Lydia never heard her coin land. There was no *plop*, or *clink*, to signify the end of its journey. Eventually, she became convinced that the coin was still falling – that it might fall forever.

Birds resumed chirping; leaves resumed rustling. The moment didn't feel so magical anymore.

She kicked the dirt and turned on her heel to leave.

'Where do you think you're going?' a voice asked.

Startled, Lydia spun back around to see a boy sitting on the edge of the well. Or at least… he looked like a boy. Though his amber eyes gleamed almost cat-like from the shadows. He was draped in black, aside from a shocking crimson blazer.

She couldn't stop gawking at his smile.

There was something in the way it curled – as though there was nothing in the world that he wouldn't find amusing.

'Where did you come from?' she asked.

The boy's smile broadened. 'Oh, here and there.'

She regarded him carefully, then glanced at the well. 'Are you the spirit?'

The boy raised an eyebrow but didn't deign to answer. Instead, he reached into his blazer pocket and pulled out a flash of silver.

'Hey, that's mine!' Lydia exclaimed.

'No, it's *my* wish. *You* gave it to me,' he grinned, then hopped off the well to stand opposite her.

For the first time that evening, Lydia felt something akin to fear. Her heart popped like a bubble in her chest.

He stood so very, very close.

She had never seen a boy with such long lashes before.

'No one in the world has everything,' the boy said quietly. 'You're going to have to be more specific.'

Lydia didn't have specifics, though. She just had a hole in her chest that she desperately wanted to fill.

'I want everything,' she said simply.

The boy smirked. 'What will you give me in return?'

Lydia opened her mouth, then closed it again.

The boy laughed and rolled the coin over his knuckles. It vanished. 'Let's play a game. You're going to come up with a wish for me – a *proper* wish – and I'm going to think of a suitable payment. Doesn't that sound fair?'

It did.

She held out her hand. 'Deal.'

The boy took a step closer and, ignoring her outstretched hand entirely, pressed his lips against hers. There was a hazy scent of earth... the faintest taste of salt.

It was quick.

Too quick? Or not quick enough? She couldn't tell.

'Deal,' the boy said.

Then he was standing on the well again, his red blazer flailing behind him as he jumped into its depths. Just like the coin, there was no sound to imply that he ever reached the bottom. No *plop* or *thud* or *crack*.

He had taken the coin, stolen a kiss, and then he had gone.

Lydia Wild peered into the darkness of the wishing well. Its never-ending night seemed suddenly oh-so-inviting.

She wondered where the boy with the long eyelashes had gone.

She wondered whether she could follow him.

She wondered if she could get her wish back...

She glanced around the woods. The leaves had stopped moving, and the branches had stopped swaying. There was not a sound to be heard.

It was as though the trees were watching her – waiting for her to make a move.

She stared back into the well; there was a tugging in the pit of her stomach and an itching in the centre of her palms.

Taking a deep breath, Lydia Wild tilted forward... and let herself fall.

* * *

It ended, as many stories often do, with a girl in the woods.

But girls don't tend to stay girls forever. They grow up, they change, they become something more.

The girl in the woods was rumoured to have golden eyes. It was whispered that she wore a silver coin around her neck and hypnotised lost souls with its shine. When she laughed, wolves howled.

Of course, to the people of the town, it was all just silly superstition.

Yet if they were to listen closely on a quiet, crimson-hued night, they would hear the creak and sigh of the trees. They would hear a name carried on the back of the wind...

Wild, Wild, Wild.

SOON MAY

LEAH ARMSTRONG

Soon May will just be a month,
left in the past because my watch ticks by and
not a reminder of a lost love.

The yellow daisies and fresh breeze,
turns to deep oranges and crisp leaves,
soon May will just be a month.

I won't shake in my room at the thought
of you and the tablets I take are
not a reminder of a lost love.

My heart won't panic
when it hears your voice and
soon May will just be a month.

I will meet new people who don't
make me cry and my teardrops will be happy
not a reminder of a lost love.

A year will pass
and the daisies will bloom.
Soon May will just be a month,
not a reminder of a lost love.

BIRTHRIGHT

PKL

We are born soaking wet and screaming,
raging at our mother,
and her holy river womb.

We are born, washed and cleansed,
free from her cyclical sacrifice,
with our choices our own.

And she weeps.

Oh, how she weeps,
because this righteous baptism
will not shield forever.

We daughters -
we will never stay clean.

Our mothers' sins, the sins against our mothers,
will become our own eventually,
despite the way we try to cling to the rage we were birthed in.

OMNISCIENT, HE

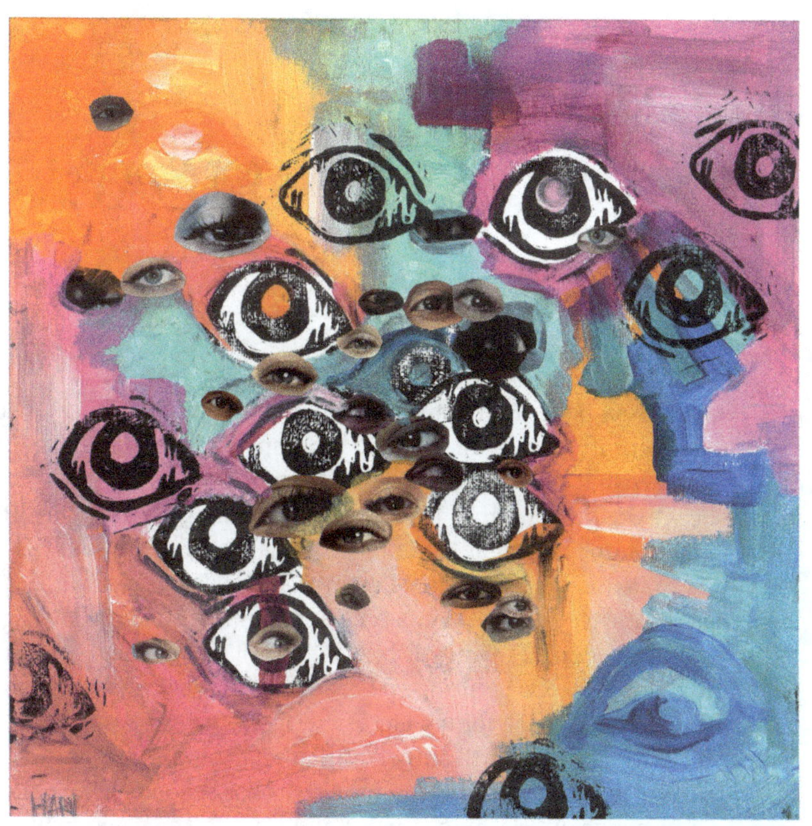

HARVEY JONES

'Being queer, there's always a feeling you're being watched. Like you're a spectacle, or somebody's waiting to catch you out somehow.'

CELESTIAL DELICACY

JOE HESTER

The rain was pouring; it was a complete downfall. The lake was spitting profusely as the raindrops impacted on the surface. Mickey looked out at the dark skyline tinged slightly blue, almost eerily. Yet it was just another typical winter evening in the heart of December. It didn't matter about taking his clothes off at this point; he was already soaking to the bone. Mickey took one deep breath, filling his lungs to capacity with all his might, before immediately jumping off the wooden boarding beneath him into the lake, submerging his body fully, only to appear tilting his head slightly backwards with a beaming grin on his face for a gasp of air, from the shock of the icy water. His perfect white teeth shined as if everything weighing on his shoulders appeared to be forgotten for a few bliss seconds before the irritation of his heavy clothing catapulted him into the water, which brought him back to reality rather quickly, weighing his body down. Snapping out of it, Mickey uses his body strength, along with a hint of adrenaline coursing through his veins, to pull himself out of the water onto the slippery wooden boards.

Around the perimeter of the lake is a thick, bushy treeline and soil banks, which is accompanied by a dimly lit cabin where Mickey spends most of his time if he's not at the farmhouse ten minutes down the close-by dirt road. Whilst his soaking wet clothes began to freeze in the crisp winter air, sharp shivering quickly greeted his damp body, prompting Mickey to sit down cross-legged. Inhaling slowly to catch his breath and regulate his breathing, a peculiar sight is caught by the bottom left corner of Mickey's eye. To his surprise, in the midst of the rough downpour, the grassy moist soil bank to his left has formed a very small crevice about the size of his palm and roughly half a finger deep within the dirt containing a tiny amount of rainwater sitting remarkably untouched, not at the worry of overflowing due to a fortunate leaf directly above the hole protecting it. It wasn't the water that caught Mickey's eye; there was a slight white glint and reflection from the crevice standing out to his curious eye.

On his hands and knees, Mickey takes two strides towards the peculiar situation, and it becomes evident that what he saw, about the size of a bouncy ball, was a clump of what looks like frog spawn, placed seemingly untouched, directly in the middle of the dirt crevice, puzzling Mickey immediately as the current climate is impossible to habitat these eggs, so he thought. Confusion spreads across his face as he inspects almost cautiously with squinted eyes.

'How can this be?' muttered Mickey.

As an outdoor kid growing up, he knew enough about nature and agriculture to understand the current perplexing situation at present wasn't quite right. This wasn't a warm, humid pond in the middle of summer; it's as freezing as Alaska out by the lake in the dead of winter. Turning back around to see the cabin, Mickey dashes a short distance towards it and flings open the wooden door. Still dripping wet, without a care in the world, he begins to rummage through all sorts of junk in the cupboards and shelves frantically, making a big mess along the way. After chucking nets, lightbulbs, and dusty books over both shoulders, he stops suddenly to regain his composure, brushing his soaked, long, dark hair backwards with his two hands, starting at his forehead and ending once he reaches the back of his scalp. Shaking his hands dry, Mickey opens a set of brown oak drawers, which were directly below the cupboards, and grins lightly as he is greeted with the item he was searching for – a glass jar. Laying in the middle of the draw, surrounded by pens and cloths, was the first piece of Mickey's cunning plan.

Despite it being late, his sole mission before getting into dry clothes and hitting the hay was to preserve and nurture his finding by the lake. With nobody to tell him otherwise, surrounded by his own thoughts, Mickey picks up the jar in his left hand and begins walking at pace, back through the door that had been left open just a few minutes previously. Not intimidated by the windy frostiness, his fixation on a sporadic encounter was a testament to his character, appearing that it was his duty to help and nurture his new discovery, providing a sense of care. Approaching the crevice again, Mickey kneels towards the small hole and takes a few more steps until he's right next to the frog spawn, still peacefully untouched and unaware of the harsh surroundings. Mickey pops open the jar, which takes a couple of tries to get the lid off as the air pressure inside probably hasn't had a release in a good few years. Mickey begins to gently scoop up the spawn into the jar, along with a small amount of water filling the jar about halfway. Once Mickey returns to the cabin, he places the now spawn-filled jar beside the window ledge and forces two holes using a nearby screwdriver on the top of the lid for airflow and oxygen circulation.

Worn out from the evening's events, Mickey finally replaces his damp clothing with warm ones and wraps himself in a dark blue cotton blanket for the night as he lays down in the corner of the cabin in his makeshift den consisting of old clothes and cotton blankets. His eyes slowly drifted closed, yet ears still perked, paying close attention to the spitting raindrops bouncing off the wooden roof and the single glass window beside the door. Just as the contemplation of tonight's events begins to register and process in Mickey's mind, his breathing begins to slow, and he drifts asleep, rather relaxed, in the company of his newfound piece of nature in mysterious circumstances. Silence finally falls, during the time Mickey is asleep with just the slight whistling in the distance from the wind. The brisk sun begins to rise in the early hours of the morning, picking up speed in its elevation as the minutes go by.

Peaceful mornings are a regular occurrence in Otis, only interrupted by high-pitched tweets of the local birds inhabiting their local familiar trees and bushes. Occasionally, the perceived sound of someone swimming in the lake is startling, only to witness harmless rabbits traipsing across the shallow edges before running back into the forest, rustling leaves along the way. By the time morning dusk has been and gone, Mickey's eyes are already bolted open, accompanied by his body, raring to go and attack the day new day. Squinting his eyes and turning his head, the almost pristine frogspawn from the evening before lay rather innocently, glistening within its new glass home as if it was just meant to be. Peacefully. The short moment of bliss was swiftly cut short; a peculiar bubbling began to sizzle from the jar with the spawn inside.

Mickey turned his attention immediately to the noise on his right. A sharp purple light captured the cabin entirely, stumbling Mickey back a few steps. The wind whistled as loud as hungry wolves outside the cabin – a deep, dark resentment built in the pit of his stomach. Something wasn't right. The delicate spawn had changed, now frothing at the brim and overspilling onto the wooden floor. Mickey runs for the door. Locked. Something's holding Mickey captive as his heart gushes twice the amount of blood to his tense organs. Before he could squeak, the frog spawn exploded gigantically. White noise, white everything. Mickey was no longer in the cabin.

'Where am I? why are you doing this to me?' Mickey cries into nothingness.

A figure appears. Tall, slender and abnormal. It's not human, it's not anything. Mickey screams for his mother.

'You were teleported here in a rift. My rift.' The figure tells Mickey in a robotic voice.

'Who are you?' Mickey mutters.

A pause that felt like a lifetime among the pure white nothingness ensured.

The distorted figure inched closer. 'Mickey. I am you.'

ORSEN NAKATUDDE-AYOOLA

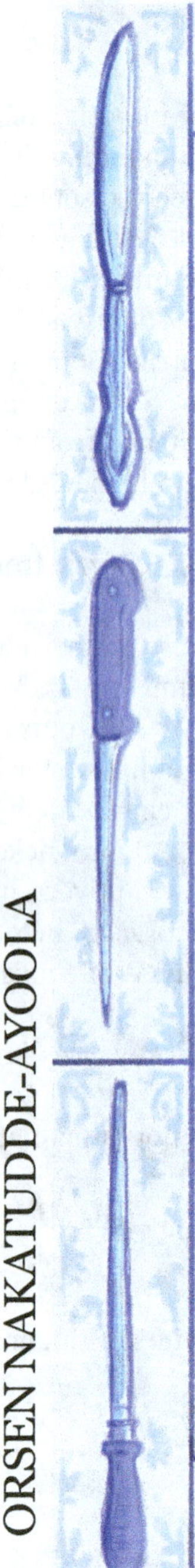

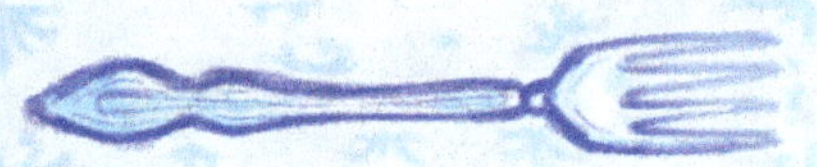

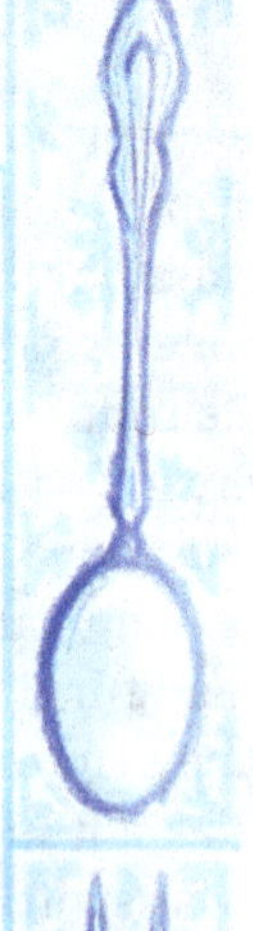

Palatable Vessel

Tonight, I host dinner,
My grand debut.
From their plates, I shall view
My guests, my consumers, and there is much to review.
They are picky eaters, you see, to feed them is tough.
They are waiting — wanting — and I'm not yet enough.

My body — a sculpture — myself — the sculptor.
Armed with my tools, I shall carve myself
Into a piece so artful they cannot refuse.
Skilfully, I slice at my greatest shame.
When the dinner bell rings, they must stare in awe.
Which is why I cleave at my jaw.

Beauty isn't skin deep.
For me, this is true.
So blemished, so marred,
My complexion is tarred.
And so they see my real appeal,
My skin, I must peel.

The worst of my flaws, I keep close to my chest.
My bosom outshines the worst of the rest.
Too saggy, not round,
Not a perk to be found.
Leavened them, I did, with a cleaver quite grand.
Now they sit on a platter and can be eaten by hand.

As the hour strikes close, the feast is due.
Hurry, I must, to be late is taboo.
So I carve at my haunches,
Whittle away at my waist,
Trim down my thighs,
For there is no time to waste.

Soon, they'll devour me with utmost zeal.
My body — the ingredients — what remains — their meal.
On platters, on trays,
On plates to be served.
When my work here is done, they shall finally say:
"What a palatable vessel! Eat dinner, we may!"

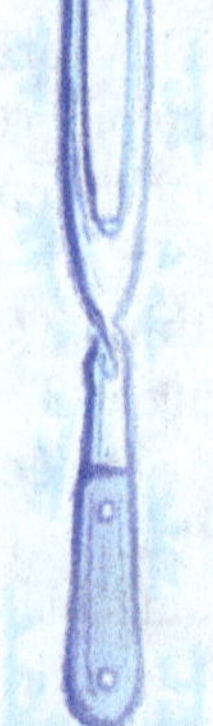

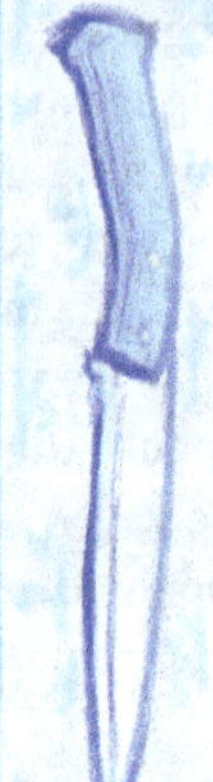

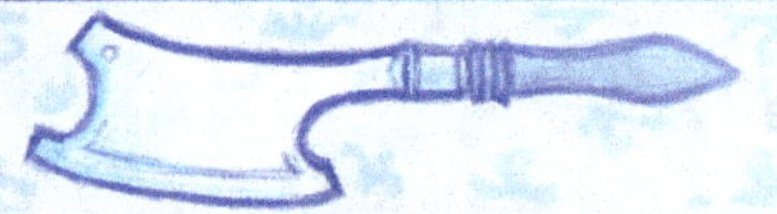

THE LIGHT AND HER FLOWERS

ZENON TEASDALE

the light and her
flowers, never grown
light stolen from night
by moon, his sun,
her life in her hands
tempted by moonlight, i
am bound to words
by rite, night and half-light,
moonlight shines like
sister sunlight for the
sun never changed,
she brings the sun
to its knees.

GUNSHOT, GO

PKL

Hell when he's touching you, and hell when he's not. The town vultures watch you wander from the porch. Didn't they know? Didn't they tell you so? Girl, he was never any good. But they still won't make eye contact with you in the store with their husbands and children and daughters, as if they've never loved something with the power to destroy and birthed his successors - a life sentence to a jukebox jingle.

Red, thick and only seven dollars a bottle for the forgiveness of every sin ever imagined - it will warm and keep you, as God promised, as God failed, as the world looked upon the purple-blue-grey-red of your youth and turned away. It's sour and burnt, and you must get your teeth fixed one day, since you lost the bottom right to an argument.

It's disapproval all-round, a celebration of 'not-me's' and 'never-my-girl', and your mother being right, always right, digging into you at the beginning like a serrated blade and twisting you farther away rather than closer. You never did figure out how to stop the bleeding, how to save the bank, how to collect and patch up the crimson.

Dirty, dirty, dirty. Unclean and bruised. Good for nothing but roadkill, but dead, but soaking through your clothes and making a mess of it all. It was late, and he wasn't home, and your things packed themselves and now you are so, so alone. You promised yourself to so many men and so many gods and so many ideas of safety and personhood that never came and will never come there.

On Sunday, will they ask where you are?

Will he even notice that you're not there until tomorrow, when he needs his baby, his love, his angel, his punching bag? In the early morning sunshine, with his headache and yours coming, will he notice?

It's a long walk to a new home and a long climb to a new mountain and it's now or never, do or die, the watchful streetlights and the eye of your Protector and the stiff ladies on their swing chairs. It's the suffocating late heat and the bugs and you.

Your dirty knees and your tangled hair and your bloodied lips and the tugging in your ribcage to *run run run run run run run run run run run run run run run run run*

run run run run run run run run run run run run run run runrunrun run run

runrunrunrunrunrunrunrunrunrunrunrun

ART

BLOSSOM CAMPBELL

She's sitting across the room from me, uncomfortably. Mere feet away from me, yet I've never felt such a great distance between us. As I look at her, look into her eyes, golden like pools of honey, I see great hurt; she's upset with me. Pretty as a picture, her face full of colour, blues, purples, reds. And brown hair like buried soil flowing down past her shoulders, shimmering in the dark green tint of the basement. She's upset with me, so I try to explain to her again. She sits there and listens without saying a word. Fine. Good, pictures aren't supposed to talk, art is not supposed to move. But I don't like that she's upset with me, I don't like that she doesn't understand when I try to explain. If only she could see herself through my eyes, how incredibly perfect she's become. I get up and walk towards her, her golden eyes widen. There's dust in the air that makes it hard to breathe and hazes the view of the basement. I walk barefoot across the cold, stained, stone floor, mainly red and grey, with the occasional sprouts of green where unwanted moss and weeds have forced their way through tiny cracks and sprouted like parasites claiming the basement floor. An icy streak courses through me as the autumn draught sneaks inside the room, chilling me to my core. The yellow of the sun has left for today and in its place is the dark and bitter September night. I reach my hand out towards her face, and she flinches away; she's still upset with me. I touch her arm and can feel her shaking, she too must be cold. After all, she's not wearing much, and what little clothing she does have on is ripped and dirty, barely clinging to her shivering limbs. The chair she's sitting in looks uncomfortable. It's wooden and unstable, like a painter's easel. I wish she would stop shaking, so I go over to the mantelpiece and get her a blanket. It's thin and slightly torn at one end, but it will help. The fire pit beneath is white and black with ash, dull lifeless colours. That will have to change. Above the mantelpiece are the remains of an old and once beautiful painting. I remember seeing it for the first time a few years back, when it still had some life and colour in it. In the painting lay a man and a woman in a field, surrounded by the greenest of grass. The girl in the painting had long, strawberry red hair, with the occasional braids that have been neatly twisted and decorated with beads and shiny clips. Her dress was white and flowy, patterned with pink and orange flowers that blended with the scenery. She's pretty. She was pretty. The man in the painting faces her, with blue denim dungarees and a white vest underneath. And messy hair that's covered by his pale straw hat. From the side of his mouth, you can just about see the hay stalk that he's chewing; the ladies must love that. The boy and the girl lay there surrounded by trees and birds and other wildlife, under a blue sky and a golden sun. What a beautiful painting it used to be. Time has passed since the first time I saw it. Today I'm gazing at it without the same awe I once had. What was once strawberry red is a dull beige; what was once blue denim is now washed-out grey. What was once a beautiful, one could even say perfect, painting has been ruined with time. I look away from the painting now and into the mirror beside it, it's dusty and old and smashed. I raise my fist to it; the red on my hands matches the red on the glass. I turn in a hurry and walk back over to her, almost tripping over the axe in the middle of the floor. I raise my arm to wrap the blanket round her and she flinches again. This will make her warmer, then she can stop shaking and loosening the duct tape. And that's important for when she's upset with me. I rip it off of her mouth and she lets out a muffled moan.

'If you start screaming again, it's going back on.'

I'm trying to reason with her, because I don't want to fight; she knows this, she must know why I'm doing this. I care about her. I'm doing this *for* her.

I have to show her I care, show her all I've done to her. For her. I grab one of the shards of glass that's lying on the floor beneath the mirror, the biggest I could find, and hold it in front of her face. She screams as the sharp piece moves closer to her. I squeeze the shard in my hand until my hands are wet.

'Look!' I shout with excitement. 'Look at all I've done! All for you!'

Her eyes turn wet as she stares in astonishment at what she has become. For I have painted her face with colours galore.

For red; I pierced her skin; such beautiful blood ran in streams down her face, the colour of the sweetest, most crisp apples, the most astounding roses.

For purple; I beat and bruised her, vibrant and sporadic shapes of all sizes and shades have freckled her face like plums and grapes in the summer.

For yellow; I burnt her skin with incredible flames that match her fiery spirit, tongues of fire, yellow and orange golden as the setting sun.

Now for blue; the bathtub is ready.

I must drown her in the bluest and coldest of waters, till her face is in the sky, only then will she be still. The perfect picture.

For I am the artist, and she is my canvas; it is my duty to restore her colours.

INTO THE FLOW_01

ANNIE HARRIS

She fell back into the great roots and felt thick,
green moss squash against her.
She heard:
A ripple becomes a trickle
becomes a tide becomes a flow,
carving channels through sands of time...
The tree said, do you know,
water never dies? Life flows eternal
in each drop. Do you know...
While you choke and gasp,
at the heart of our earth is a forest,
a forest that breathes for us all.
At the heart of the forest is a Great Tree,
the Mother Tree, 'Mente', bearing
all in her branches. She will show you
how to live as intended, lives within lives,
rising up through the canopy in communion with Spirit.
Approach with reverence, her roots run deep.
                    She shows how to nurture
And receive; she knows **to survive** we need her and she needs
us. She is the Mother Tree, Mente,
root and limb, because and of and for, all this.
She says, lay your brow upon my mossy roots and dream,
I will show you how it is.
She says, walk with spirit now.

ROMULUS & REMUS

HAN ILETT

It's stupid, but I'm jealous of your hair,
how Dad lets you part it to one side.
How he gave you his jacket to wear.

I watch you press your shirts with care;
your reflection in the mirror, flat, brown-eyed.
My chest aches. I'm jealous of your hair.

In our bedroom that night, I throw up a prayer,
a lie. *I trust you know who I am inside.*
On the hook, that jacket for you to wear.

Mum says we make a perfect pair;
I close my eyes. You sneer, say something snide.
I'm really fucking jealous of your hair.

Dad fixes me firmly beneath his icy glare:
you could be someone good if you tried.
He gave you his favourite jacket to wear.

I could lay these words, myself, my soul bare,
if it weren't for the blue heat of my pride.
It's stupid, but I'm jealous of your hair,
how Dad never gave me his jacket to wear.

NATURE OF THE WALK

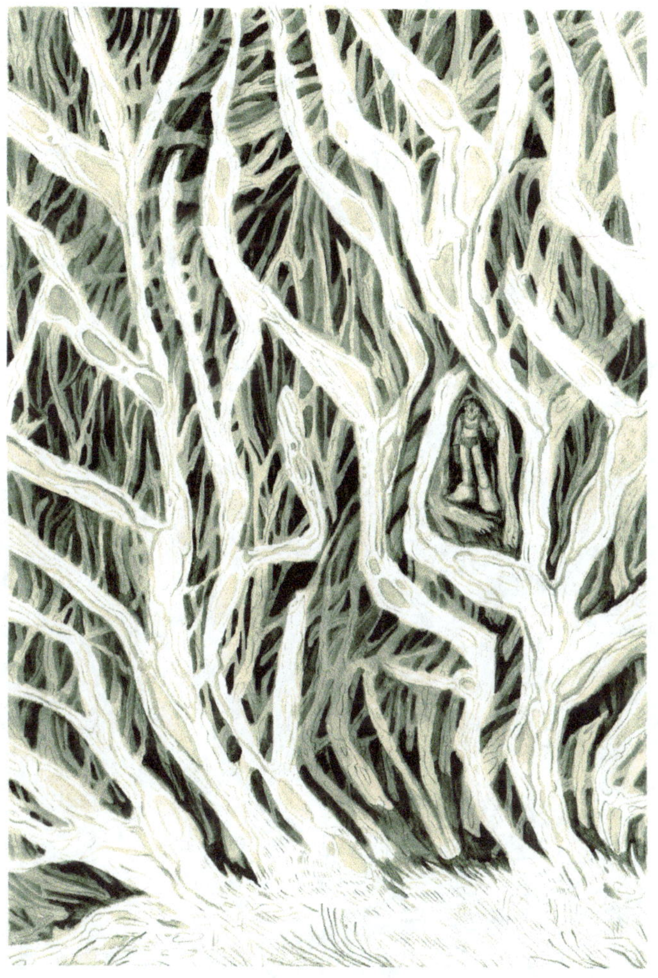

EYLUL OGUZ

'Being out in nature reminds one of their insignificance, one's body always seems small relative to the infinitely large landscape.'

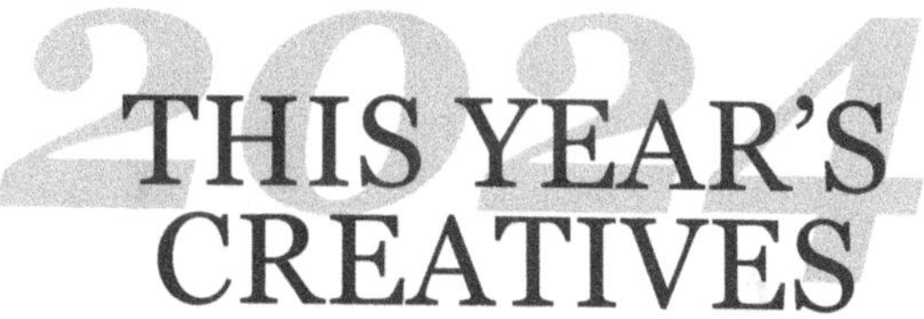

THIS YEAR'S CREATIVES

JAD H. AL-SHARA'A
An overly ambitious young Syrian international law student interested in literature and seeking resolve in making his thoughts and emotions heard through words.

LEAH ARMSTRONG
Leah Armstrong is a current MA Creative Writing and Publishing student at Kingston university. She loves sudoku, coffee and queer literature.

SOFIA CAMARA-MARTINS
Sofia is a Portuguese student influenced by the complexity of Russian literature due to its historical reference and its revolutionary and unconventional features that break literary boundaries. She also depicts feminist themes in poetry and prose.

BLOSSOM CAMPBELL
Blossom is a first-year KU student for creative writing and film. She wants to be a screenwriter and to direct films in the future. She loves the idea that she can channel emotions into her work that can be felt and experienced by the audience.

NOAH CHANDLER
Noah is a Creative Writing BA student from the States. His writing is often interested in facets of American culture and imagery. 'I90 to I10' was partially inspired by his own travels through America, but mainly by the ever-moving seasonal workers he met while working in Alaska.

REBECCA CHANDLER
Rebecca Chandler is a queer, disabled poet and performer who will not stop writing about stars. Her poetry ranges from the mythical and fantastical to impassioned discussion of disability, neurodivergence, poverty and mental health.

JOSHUA CICCONE
Joshua is currently studying English Literature at KU. He is a science fiction, fantasy and crime fan, but he reads everything he can get his hands on. He was previously published in Kingston RiPPLE 2023.

JULIA COLOMBO
Julia Colombo grew up in a small town in Western New York where very little ever happens, and that encourages her to pay attention to the seemingly insignificant. She takes small moments, details, conversations and images and expresses their gravity in her writing.

JOJO CONNORS
Jojo Connors is a young, aspiring author from the UK studying Journalism and Media at Kingston University. When they aren't studying, they are focused on writing pieces for their website and creating art. They can often be seen carrying a Discworld novel with them; they one day hope to write their novels.

IMOGEN CROCKFORD
Imogen is currently studying for a master's degree in Creative Writing and Publishing. Much of her work is inspired by photographers and visual poets. She also loves artists and writers who mix medians and formats. She enjoys working on digital projects, experimenting with software and implementing sketches and photographs into her work.

BIANCA FOGAH

Bianca is an MA student in Creative Writing who loves to explore the emotional impact of stories. She enjoys the challenge of crafting narratives and exploring what makes a story truly compelling. Her favourite genres include crime fiction, psychological fiction, mystery and young adult literature.

CONNI LAURA GROVES

Conni is a lesbian, working-class poet from Portsmouth, studying drama at KU. Her work navigates the realms of queer identity and womanhood, serving as a testament to the nuanced tapestry of existence. Often informed by the vibrant hues of religious imagery, she delves into the intricate dance between faith and self-discovery.

ANNIE HARRIS

Annie believes in the great potential for awakened environmental consciousness, and after many years as a journalist, travel writer and educational content provider, she is seeking more creative ways of telling that tale. She is inspired by the art of storytelling and uses these to fight for clean water and air.

JOE HESTER

Joe is a second-year creative writing student, and his writing has a particular emphasis on landscape and scenery to achieve the ambience he desires. He loves transforming regular life situations into special experiences with zero boundaries in his fiction.

HAN ILETT

Han is a part-time KU student, part-time teacher. They write poetry and literary fiction about queer life and love. Their work explores how we use objects to express and cement our identities, and how beauty and romance can be found in the most unlikely of places.

HARVEY JONES

Harvey is a Welsh mixed media artist with a love of lino cutting and collage. He is inspired mainly by pop art and its colour palettes and enjoys using them in a surreal context. He hopes that viewers can find their own meanings in his paintings.

STEVE KENT

Steve, former President of the KU Creative Writing Society, is a final year Politics PhD student, focusing his research on the themes of estrangement and appeasement. He enjoys writing historical fiction and science fiction in his limited spare time.

CHIA-YING LIN

Chia-Ying is an illustrator from Taiwan, driven by a passion for the inner world, vintage aesthetics, ancient myths and the enigmatic allure of astrology. Her art is a journey into unravelling the mysteries of the unknown. With each illustration, she aims to provide viewers with a unique perspective, inviting them to explore the captivating realms of her influences and interests.

HUIYIN LIN

Huiyin is a student from the Department of Illustration Animation. Her work is about her original character. He is a killer with a tragic experience and is now the lead singer and guitarist of the band. Huiyin wants to create a vivid character through painting.

SYLVIA LIU

Sylvia is a fashion designer, stylist, and soon-to-be curator. Growing up in Taiwan, with a rich and diverse religious tradition background, Sylvia is interested in death and the afterlife, Taoism, Buddhism, Western paganism and gothic culture. She believes everything is connected, and those practices are all driven by people's emotions.

RACHEL MATTHEWS

Rachel is a part-time student, part-time bookseller and writer with an unhealthy addiction to coffee and chocolate eclairs. She lives with her husband and dog in the not-so-sunny Worthing. When not crying over her laptop, she can be found combing charity shops for books or watching Gilmore Girls for the gazillionth time.

ALEX MCALPINE

Alex grew up in the exotic lands of suburban America, daydreaming about life elsewhere. Her love of sci-fi and fantasy grew after being bitten by a radioactive book. She is currently studying publishing and creative writing at KU and is working on her first novel.

KARINA MIRIKLIS

Karina is a Curating Contemporary Design MA student, originally from Melbourne, Australia. She immensely enjoys heralding the work of others, including strolling through the myriad of art galleries and museums London has to offer.

ORSEN NAKATUDDE-AYOOLA

Orsen is a Black Transgender writer and artist. He loves writing poetry and short stories centred around Black and Queer experiences in various genres, settings and time periods. He also adores merging storytelling with his passion for drawing.

SONATA NEZNAMY

Sonata, originally from Dallas, Texas, has been creating since she can remember. Her work can have a melancholic, heavy air, but despite her Wednesday Addams exterior, inside Sonata is more akin to Buddy the Elf and just wants to enjoy the beautiful gift of existing.

EYLUL OGUZ

Eylul is a Turkish artist pursuing her master's in Illustration. Her work focuses on figure and environment and what meanings come from their relations in an image.

SHANAYE NICOLE PEACOCK
Shanaye is began writing poetry as a mechanism to express her emotions, her way to vent and unload. Her motivation is to reach out to people who can relate to or find comfort or even feel less alone. Writing plays and screenwriting has been her gateway to delve into a fiction world that she can control, to stir away from her experiences.

JULES PENDRAGON
Jules is an elusive fantasy writer who thrives in shadows. With a penchant for magic, she transforms the mundane, infusing whimsy into our monotonous world through her captivating stories.

P K L
This is P K L's second time being published through the Ripple anthology. She is mainly inspired by aestheticist American culture and dreams of going to Texas one day. They love exploring religion, trauma and emotion through horror stories and poetry. She is autistic and navigates the world through art.

JULES SHIPTON
Jules is currently studying fine art at Kingston University and has been a writing for decades. Jules' concerns are the marginalised, unspoken truths that society sweeps to the edge or capitalises.

ZENON TEASDALE
Zenon likes to think he is an Artangel. His work isn't for the eyes, but for the soul. He looks to push creative boundaries, to invent and create, particularly in the horror/sci-fi genres. His life is in his work, and, with that, he lives forever. Death is but a temporary feeling.

BETTY WATERS
Writing has been a passion for Betty since she was a child. It's always helped her define and express her truth. She had a handful of children's books published in the early 2000s before she had kids. Now she is an MA student in creative writing, (Distance Learning).

2024

ACKNOWLEDGEMENTS

In the rhythmic flow of creativity, RiPPLE has surged forward, embodying the collaborative spirit of KU students. This anthology is not just a collection of words and pictures on paper; it's a testament to the dedication, passion and synergy of many talented individuals.

To the judging team, your discerning eyes ensured the selection of outstanding pieces. To the editing team, your meticulous work polished each gem to perfection. To the design team, your exceptional skills crafted a visually stunning experience. And to the marketing team, your efforts ensured RiPPLE reached every corner of our campus and beyond, not only with social media but also with podcasts and workshops.

A special shout out goes out to my phenomenal head of marketing, Leah Armstrong, whose innovative ideas and tireless dedication played a pivotal role in promoting RiPPLE to new heights. And to my brilliant art director, Karina Miriklis, whose keen artistic eye was invaluable. I truly could not have done this without you two.

Detailing everyone's names and tasks would demand an extended acknowledgment. However, I wish to express my gratitude to key contributors: my meticulous senior copyeditor, Reyna Cox; my genius cover designer, Imogen Crockford; and my creative page designers, Rose Edwards and Chaya Chudasama.

I also extend my deepest appreciation to Emma Tait, our esteemed course leader for MA Publishing, for her unwavering guidance throughout the entire process. Her expertise and encouragement have been the driving force behind RiPPLE's continued success. Thank you for placing your trust in me.

Celebrating our 20th edition, this anthology marks a milestone as the first to feature a cover adorned with student artwork, reflecting the vibrant creativity within our university community.

As co-producer of a groundbreaking new feature, I am also thrilled to introduce our inaugural audiobook version, accessible through a QR code. I thank my co-producer Verónica S Rodríguez García and my audio editor Ally McAlpine for making this possible. This marks a new era for RiPPLE, adding an extra dimension to the reader's experience, making literature not just something to read but something to hear and feel.

And of course, no anthology is complete without the voices of our gifted writers, poets and artists. It is your words, verses and visual expressions that breathe life into these pages, creating a tapestry that captivates and inspires.

Last but not least, a heartfelt thank you to you, our dear reader. Your support fuels our commitment and passion to nurturing and showcasing literary and artistic endeavours.

Here's to the power of words and art that makes RiPPLE a beacon of talent and imagination. Cheers to the 20th edition and many more to come!

Julieta Pereyra
Managing Editor, RiPPLE 2024

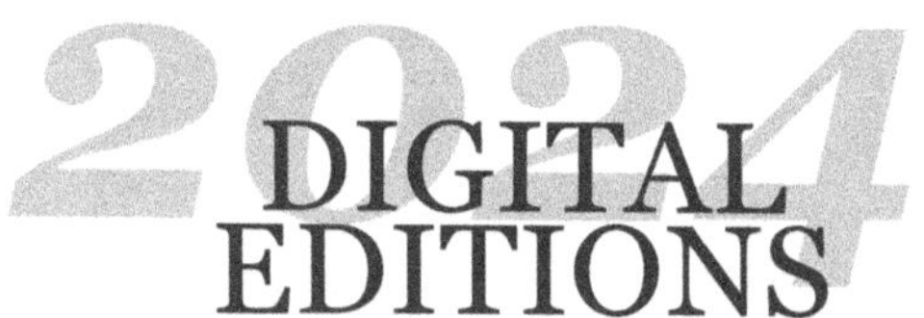

We are thrilled to offer accessible editions to RiPPLE this year. Introducing our latest additions – audiobook and eBook editions! Our readers can now immerse themselves in the rich variety of short stories, poems and art pieces with the convenience of digital formats. Whether you prefer to listen on the go or curl up with your favorite electronic device, RiPPLE is now more accessible than ever. Join as we embark on this exciting journey, making literature inclusive and available to all.

The QR code below will take you to the launch pad for these editions, as well as any other information you may be looking for about RiPPLE and KU Press.

2024

ABOUT KU PRESS

Kingston University Press has been publishing high-quality commercial and academic titles for over ten years. Our list has always reflected the diverse nature of the student and academic bodies at the university in ways that are designed to impact on debate, to hear new voices, to generate mutual understanding and to complement the values to which the university is committed.

Increasingly the books we publish are produced by students on the Kingston School of Art MA courses, often working with partner organisations to bring projects to life. While keeping true to our original mission, and maintaining our wide-ranging backlist titles, our most recent publishing focuses on bringing to the fore voices that reflect and appeal to our community at the university as well as the wider reading community of readers and writers in the UK and beyond.

@KU_press

This book was edited, designed, typeset and produced by students on the Kingston School of Art MA courses at Kingston University, London.

To find out more about our hands-on, professionally focused and flexible MA and BA programmes please visit:

www.kingston.ac.uk
www.kingstonpublishing.wordpress.com
@kingstonjourno

www.ingramcontent.com/pod-product-compliance
Lightning Source LLC
La Vergne TN
LVHW020056110826
845155LV00022B/87